CATCHING TROUT

David,

Please accept this with my compliments. I've really enjoyed fishing with you & look forward to your next trip. Tight lines!

Regards,

Graeme Marshall

CATCHING TROUT

By
Les Hill & Graeme Marshall

Line Drawings By
Grant Winter

Les Hill

Graeme Marshall

The
Halcyon
Press

Published by

The Halcyon Press.

C.P.O. Box 360, Auckland, New Zealand.

A division of

Halcyon Publishing Ltd.

ISBN 0 908685 80 7

Typesetting: Typeset Graphics Ltd
Printed in Hong Kong through Colorcraft Limited

CONTENTS

Acknowledgements

I am indebted to many people who have helped me in various ways to complete my contribution to this book and other writings.

First, I'm grateful to my father who introduced me to fishing and taught me the value of patience and perseverance. My mother always had a meal ready for tired fishermen and provided a warm, quiet room and countless cups of coffee during hours of writing.

I'm also aware of the contribution of my many fishing friends who patiently manoeuvered themselves before my camera. In addition, the ones I introduced to fishing know they contributed much material for me to draw upon. But now they catch as many fish as I do and, ironically, remind me when I err!

In this book and in *Stalking Trout*, we have worked as a team. Part of our team, and contributing immeasurably to both books has been Grant Winter, illustrator. Our thanks go to him.

— Les Hill.

My greatest debt of gratitude is to my long suffering family who have sacrificed outings while Dad picked away at his word processor.

I also salute my co-author, angling companion and great friend who never despaired even when yet another deadline went by.

— Graeme Marshall.

Introduction

In recent years, trout fishing (and fly fishing in particular) has gained increasing popularity. This growth is probably part of the trend in New Zealand away from traditional team sports, towards individual participation in a wide variety of activities and it's probably a part, too, of an increasing interest in the outdoors.

Some accomplished anglers have forseen the change and have set up fishing schools at fixed locations; others have shared their expertise on a more mobile basis. Some institutes, like the Polytechnics, now offer fly fishing tuition. Fishing clubs give their own help to members. Retailers have not been slow to increase their promotional efforts and even some schools, where enthusiasts teach, are making a contribution to kindling of interest and the sharing of knowledge.

We have been part of all of this and have assisted at schools and through clubs and institutes. But more importantly we have had wide experience in the practical, river bank teaching. In helping others we have learnt too, learnt a great deal. It is what we learnt while helping relative novices that we would like to pass on in this book.

The essence of our message is simple. When an angler decides to pursue fly fishing the advice of others should be sought. Others can help in the purchase of gear, rods, reels, etc., or in the wise choice of flies or nymphs. Others can lead the novice up a river and point out feeding fish — in fact they can do everything up to that point. But, from the moment a feeding fish is discovered until it is in the net, the angler is on his own. He must approach the fish himself, cast the fly, induce the take, effect a strike, fight the fish, net it and, we hope, release it.

There are libraries of books on tying flies, casting, construction of gear, where to go and so on. Repeating all that in this book would be of little value. Our aim has been to concentrate on just one aspect of angling — that is the act of capture from the time a fish has been spotted.

We hope that through this book we can assist anglers, novices in particular, to identify and solve some of their difficulties but also increase their sensitivity to the often under-estimated adversary, the trout.

As in our earlier book, *Stalking Trout*, we took responsibility for separate sections of this work so that we could write individually at our Nelson and Christchurch homes. Les Hill compiled *The First Cast*, Chapters 1 to 4 and Chapter 9 while Graeme Marshall was responsible for Chapters 5 to 8 and *The Last Cast*. As mentioned in the Acknowledgements, the drawings are by Grant Winter. Les Hill took the photographs.

The First Cast

I began fishing about 33 years ago, using a threadline. It caught few fish, yet, in leading me streamside, it no doubt guided me unwittingly through numerous valuable lessons, nurturing me in the ways of a river and the ways of a trout. My relationship with a threadline has never ceased completely. When all else fails the old friend is always there.

My association with a fly rod really began in my early teens and, as time progressed, I came closer and closer to the conclusion that the only certainty in trout fishing is that there are no certainties. Maybe that's what leads so many people into fishing, absorbs them and bonds them for life.

Yes, there are no certainties — yet one thing I am becoming more convinced about is the importance of the first cast. Some fish may tempt an angler for an hour or more, demand a dozen offerings, inspect them all before finally, inexplicably accepting one. Others may take after just two or three changes, maybe a nymph instead of dry; others still may be deceived after a handful. But many accept the first pass, the first offering — one that was right — right in fly, right in drift, right in deportment, right for taking.

It would be interesting to document the actual numbers of fish taken on the first cast compared with those taken thereafter. I'd venture the first lures nearly as many as the others together. My own experience has been that if my fly is refused the first time I regard my chances of catching the fish have been halved.

Recently, at the end of a most successful day, a fishing friend, Eden Shields, and I, while sharing a generous drink, discussed this very idea as it applied to our experiences on that particular day.

The day began, as all fishing days should, a fish apiece sighted and a fish apiece landed. Clean and tidy, almost clinical.

The river was sparkling clear, tossing along in a warm, mid-morning sun. High bushclad bluffs, reaching skywards, backed the opposite bank adding to our ease in spotting. The first fish was lying, or more correctly swaying about, over a white, sedimentary slab. How often they do this. Sometimes just the head on a downstream edge;

sometimes right over the rock as this one was. Food drifting there, rolling over the slab, must be easily seen, easy pickings.

Eden waded in behind, less than knee-deep, stripped several metres of line through a tightly buckled rod, then relaxed, ready to cast. A dry, no doubt. Eden has a little aversion to nymphs, or is it a greater affinity for flies, a hint of purity? Up it went, high in the air then forward, two or three times, gaining balance, judging distance. Once more, then down. The fly curled a little, pitched briefly in the hands of a gentle breeze, before resting wings upright. The trout, scorning its nymphs, responded immediately. Eden would be the finest fish striker I know. I must have seen him rise a hundred fish — if he has missed one I can't remember it. A style of no mercy, no hesitation.

With a more laboured, hesitant strike and less vigorous landing, I secured the next fish which fed a few metres upstream. As it was released I reflected that it too had taken, quite positively, on the first cast. All was going well.

On to the next. Eden again. Sometimes, when it's your turn to fish, conditions are just right. The trout holds in a shallow, ripply run, ripples to hide the cast and engulf the nylon. The fish feeds freely, the breeze is on your back and there's casting room aplenty. No excuses.

However, and it seems more often these days, fate creates little problems. This time Eden had a difficulty. The fish he was after was feeding in shallow, ripply water and ranging hungrily, but it was holding ahead of a large boulder and had a tongue of much faster water streaming away quickly on both its sides, creating a potential for fatal fly drag.

Two options. The first — to move forward and cast from an adjacent position. Often in this way the swift tongues can be largely avoided, but the hazard is that from side on an angler is more easily seen. Eden chose the second and safer place — directly behind, but from there he had to alter his casting technique a little. His trick was to stop the forward drive early, well above the horizontal — allowing the leader, lacking some forward power, to fall more vertical than horizontal and land in loose coils. In the time faster flow had straightened the nylon a natural drift over the fish should have been effected.

Fingers crossed, Eden prepared to cast. The final stroke was good — stopped early. His floating line snaked marginally, the leader coiled down to half its extended length. The fly landed less than a metre ahead of the fish. In the following moments I watched four things: the floating line being sucked mercilessly, by the fast flow, coils of nylon straightening rapidly, the fly drifting painfully slowly forwards and the fish lifting with due interest but devoid of haste. The trout and fly drew nearer to each other. The fish's snout lifted, but then, inevitably, the fly began to drag, tugged by taut nylon, pushing tiny waves ahead. Barely perceptible but obviously clear to the fish. No panic, it just refused and made an unhurried return to its former feeding pattern.

Eden's second cast was even better — the same fly with a longer drag-free drift, right over the trout's snout. No interest whatsoever. Naturals were still being seized freely. "A change of fly," muttered Eden. The second fly was inspected closely yet, despite a most natural ride — high, slow, enticing; rejection again. And so to a third change, then a fourth. The pattern repeated.

That first cast, that was the one. That was the one to achieve a complete, drag-free drift. Had it been so I'm sure the fish would have taken.

Much of our talk, long into that night, centred around the number of fish deceived on the first cast and the number of fish which refused our initial offering through some minute foible and were not to be tempted beyond inspection again.

The first cast. If the assumption of its importance has substance, if it offers the greatest chance of luring a feeding fish, then perhaps it deserves appropriate attention. Heed your fly choice, tread lightly and present delicately. A mindful first cast is a tribute to the trout, a tribute to its instinct and nobility. This compliment paid will reap reward.

1

Getting Ready To Cast

Ahead, maybe 20 metres away, a trout is feeding. It is unaware of your presence. It feeds so freely it offers an irresistible invitation.

Days on a river vary. Some outings will present 15 fish that way while on other days, of squall and cloud, there will be only two similar chances. Each chance is an experience worthy of "giving your best shot", to make that outstanding day one to reminisce about or that difficult day a satisfying one.

You are the intruder, you are in the fish's domain. The trout is much more familiar with the surroundings. Therefore you begin at a disadvantage. Furthermore your desire to catch the fish, although strong, is undoubtedly less powerful than the trout's instinct to survive. Beware. Treat that trout with the utmost respect. Act with extreme caution. Err on the conservative side in all that you do. Aim at avoiding offering all of those half chances of detection. Aim at total deception. If you feel that the trout can possibly get a glimpse of you — shift back, drop lower. If you feel your leader might be a fraction short, lengthen it, and so on. With an ultra-sensitive attitude to approaching the fish and to avoiding detection you will be tuned for success.

An upstream approach — from behind the fish.

Having spotted a feeding fish, your initial task is to get yourself into position to make an effective cast and present, undetected, a fly or nymph. Written or said quickly this seems a simple matter. Watch an expert and so it appears. But in fact there are many precautions a prudent angler must observe.

Observation

Firstly, you should use one of your greatest weapons — observation. Try to note the depth of water in which the fish is feeding. Is it feeding on nymphs or surface insects, or both? What distance is the trout moving from its holding position to select food? Is it feeding predominantly to one side or other? These considerations are important because the knowledge gained will affect your decisions in your next tasks — preparing the leader and selecting the fly.

A general rule I use is that a leader should be about a rod length and a half long (edging on the long side). The shorter a leader, the easier it is to cast accurately, but the closer the floating line (visible and menacing) is being placed to the fish. Another generalisation, but an important one, is that the deeper a fish feeds the longer the leader must be for safety. So, having observed the fish ahead and the depth of its holding position, you can make the necessary adjustments and prepare to attach fly or nymph.

Selecting A Fly Or Nymph

The decision you make here will again relate to your initial observations. A surface feeder deserves a dry while a nymphing fish should logically be enticed by an imitation resembling its choice. Weighted or not? How deep is it feeding? Stonefly, mayfly, caddis, beetle, damselfly, dobsonfly or what? What sort of river are you fishing on? Lowland stream or high country freestone? What time of year is it?

Again I'll offer my own simple guidelines — if you're faced with a simple fish they may work! On a high country river my first choice is usually a Stonefly or Mayfly Nymph (e.g. a Green Stonefly Nymph, size 10, or a Pheasant Tail Nymph, size 14) or a Mayfly Dry — (Dad's Favourite, size 12-14 or Kakihi Queen, size 12-14). On lowland streams mayflies and caddis flies usually get preference with the sizes generally smaller (e.g. Pheasant Tail Nymph, size 14-16, Caddis Nymph, size 14-16, Dad's Favourite Dry, size 16, or Twilight Beauty Dry, size 16).

It's very easy to become too analytical but time and experience will help you to understand more about river fauna, to be more aware of trout behaviour, to be able to read river hydrology and so on. Your choice of fly or nymph can thus be logically based, and your method of fishing fully considered. But it is important to bear in mind one ever-present factor when dealing with trout — their capricious nature and their capacity to disregard their own rules.

Last summer I spent a number of interesting days at the head of Lake Ohau. Constant north-west winds kept the local rivers muddy with snowmelt and powerful down-valley gusts created frustrating conditions. But the lake edge, approached from the windward side, offered a different prospect.

Overhead the sun shone brightly, but, down valley, the wind gusted constantly. So while the broad shallows were well lit, the surface of the lake, being rippled and chopped, allowed one to sneak inconspicuously among the grasses. Sometimes the trout themselves could be seen, but more frequently they appeared as moving shadows. Little streams and ditches trickled into the lake, emerging from deep, inviting channels, which reached lakewards, cleaving shallows and weedbeds. These were the productive spots, places oozing promise, demanding caution, guaranteeing excitement.

I'm a relative novice when it comes to lake edge fishing. I spend more time river-bound — so there's much I've yet to learn about the still water secrets. But, watching the margins of the first lake-bound channel gave me some hints. Two fish foraged to and fro and led me analytically to my fly box. One fish nosed along the muddy bed, stopping repeatedly, then occasionally nibbled among the stems of a weedbed. Snails, I surmised. The second fed aggressively, cruising gracefully for a distance then accelerating alarmingly one way then the other, then roving innocently once more. A diet of small fish?

The active one took my fancy. A small lure was smartly tied on. No need for extra weight in the shallows. Preparations complete I looked waterwards again. Not a fish in sight. Another demand of lake edge shallows — patience. There wasn't long to wait. I didn't see it approaching, despite reasonable vigilance, but suddenly the fish appeared on the fringe of the channel 15 metres away and edging closer. The three coils of line hanging loosely in my left hand were soon speeding through the guides on my rod then straightening in a low back cast. The fly plopped four metres in front of the fish. A delay of a few seconds allowed the lure to sink. Then began a slow, expectant retrieve. Expectation was as close as I got. Not a flicker of interest was shown. What now? Water boatman perhaps. They hovered and darted in abundance — in the muddy shallows in particular.

On a finer tippet I tied a tiny imitation. This too dropped handy to the fish and then twitched invitingly — or so I thought. Again no response. Not even a distant inspection.

That's where all analysis ceased. A few seasons earlier I'd been confounded similarly on the shallows of Lake Mavora. On that occasion I'd eventually succeeded with a green stonefly nymph. A green stonefly! Ever seen one in the muddy margins of a lake? Green stoneflies characteristically inhabit freestone rivers, creep beneath stones and boulders and tempt high country river trout. Yet that's what they'd taken that day — in fact, they had moved several metres to intercept them.

With that in mind my next choice was made. Wise is probably an inappropriate adjective but successful cannot be denied. The really amazing thing though is that the next four fish I cast to moved quite positively to the stonefly as soon as it dipped into the lake. Three browns and one rainbow.

The lesson is simple. While an analytical, logical approach to deceiving trout will frequently reap rewards, and is probably the most reliable way, do not become too fastidious, too reasoned in your approach, because the trout are full of surprises.

Strike Indicators

With your leader carefully measured and your fly chosen, one more decision is necessary before you proceed. If using a nymph, do you use a strike indicator?* My advice would be quite positive. The newcomers to trout fishing I've assisted have all seemed more secure and successful when aided by an indicator. When preparing their tackle they have invariably opted for one.

FOOTNOTE:

*An indicator is used when nymph fishing. Its purpose is to indicate to the angler when the nymph (which is fished beneath the water's surface) has been taken by a trout. The take shows by the unnatural stopping or hesitation of the indicator or its sudden disappearance into the water. The most common indicators are a dry fly, short lengths of wool, strips of plastic or plastic bubbles.

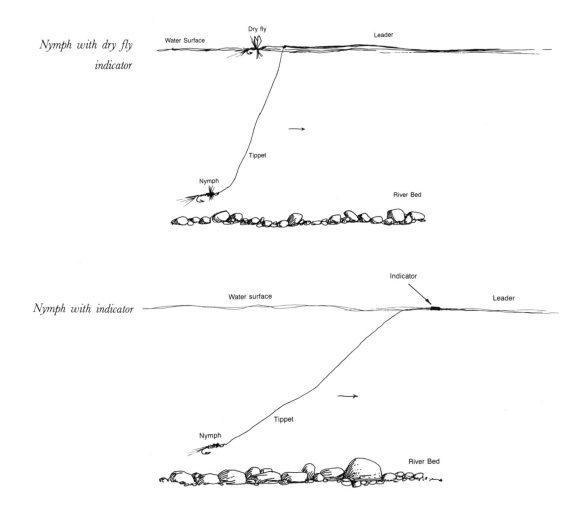

Nymph with dry fly indicator

Nymph with indicator

My first choice for an indicator is always a dry fly. I prefer it because, to me, it looks more natural than gaudy pieces of plastic. Aesthetics aside, I find that my indicator is frequently taken instead of the nymph. This happens occasionally with pieces of plastic too, but with no hook the encounter is brief. The disadvantage of a dry fly indicator is that, as a result of its being attached by a short extension of nylon at an angle to the leader, a tangle can develop. More care and skill is required in casting. There is also a limit to how far back along the leader a dry fly can be effectively attached. I'd suggest a limit of about 1.5 metres. There is no limit with other indicators.

When adding tippet material to my leader I always make provision for attaching a dry fly indicator. At the junction, where the last two pieces of nylon are joined, there are always two tails left. The normal practice is to snip these off as short as is safely possible. I snip only

one — the tippet piece. The other is left as a 12 centimetre tail. Fishing can continue with nothing attached or, if an indicator is preferred, a dry fly can be tied to this tail.

Plastic strike indicators, although causing some air resistance, affect casting only marginally. They're very visible and therefore of great assistance to a beginner who has so many skills to master, so many things to look for and is likely to welcome every crutch within grasp.

Care is needed in placing the indicator on the leader. How far should it be from your nymph? Taupo anglers, fishing with heavily weighted nymphs, probe great depths of water. Because indicators must remain visible on the surface, they tend to have theirs near the junction of leader and floating line — several metres from the nymph. Anglers fishing shallower waters however shift their indicators much closer to their nymph.

The reasoning is simple. An indicator is there to convey a message to the watchful angler. A moment's hesitation, a dip downwards, a stop, all suggest the nymph has been taken. An immediate strike is essential. Clearly, the take comes first and the indicator movement follows. If there is a great distance between nymph and indicator, any time delay because of slack line, may mean a loss of contact with the fish, an inappropriate timing of the strike — and a lost trout. The ideal is to have the indicator marginally further from the nymph than the depth of water being fished. So if a trout is feeding on the bed in a metre of water then place the indicator about 1.3 metres from the nymph.

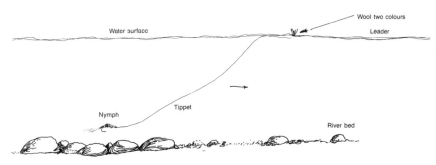

"The Nelson Guides' Technique".
Nymph with wool indicator.

"The Tony Entwistle Method".
An alternative way of attaching
a dry fly indicator between
leader and tippet.

But I'd be loath to follow this rule to the letter. If a trout is nymphing in 0.3 metres of water I would not risk landing a piece of brightly coloured plastic just above its head or immediately ahead. Rarely would my indicator be less than a metre from the nymph.

Caution

When preparing your leader and selecting and attaching your fly, be cautious. Don't make your preparations on the river bank position from which the trout was spotted. Move away, if you can, to a place where you know you can't be seen. When this is not possible some further precautions need consideration. At all times keep the rod tip low and facing downstream — away from the fish. This is particularly important while altering leaders because at that time the rod tends to get waved about. While selecting flies, turn your back to the fish. Most fly boxes, being metallic, reflect and flash. Another note of caution. What colour is that backpack? When you turn, to avoid flashing your fly box (or watch) at the fish, you may well expose a backpack, of less than subtle tones. It all seems so simple, so logical — yet I'd be embarrassed to reveal the number of trout I've scared through my stupidity, my lack of appreciation of the trout's unrelenting vigilance and caution, its will to survive. We lose our concentration often on a river, we relax and opt for short cuts. Trout never stop looking for danger. They wouldn't be there if they did!

Backpacks, flashing fly boxes and watches are not the only unnecessary signals we grant to trout. Many of the obvious errors relate to inappropriate clothing. Camo jackets and trousers suit most environments although other sombre vests in greens and browns serve wary anglers well too. The jacket or shirt is more important than the trousers because the upper body, being higher, emerges into a trout's vision first. Most anglers demonstrate an appreciation of this in their dress yet many of the same people sport hats of orange or red or with light tones beneath the peak — the very piece first visible to a trout from its lower perspective. Our hats too often bear less than subtle bands and patches while vests, carefully designed and coloured are inexplicably adorned with white material patches for conveniently holding flies.

Wearing camouflage clothing.

Our tackle too, being ahead of us while fishing, or at our side while stalking, deserves some thought. Rods and ring bindings come in a multitude of colours. Obviously the first consideration in making a choice is the rod's performance but the trimmings of non-gloss finish, dull or blending ring binding material may sway you. Many reels come in bright metallic colours, highly reflective, but a silver-sided reel can easily be dulled at little or no cost. Having selected a sombre rod and dull-toned reel, an equally conservative line would complement your tackle perfectly.

Approach with the rod away from the fish.

I can hear the odd chortle from an occasional cynic. A breast patch scaring a fish? Rod flash sending them scuttling? An orange band on a hat causing alarm? Small chances, minor signals, agreed. But if a trout had a six-centimetre square patch of white on its back or a shiny silver tail wouldn't our job of spotting it be infinitely easier? So why shouldn't the converse apply? Ask the cynic too: What percentage of the trout they see feeding do they actually catch? Fifty per cent? I doubt it. Thirty per cent? They're much better than I am. Why aren't these fish caught? Either they simply won't take or they are scared. Equally appropriately — and less easily gauged — how many feeding fish are scared without us even knowing? Many I'm sure. What scared them? A signal from a not so subtle angler.

Keep the fish in sight whenever possible.

Ready To Move — Almost!

Your tackle is prepared for casting — a leader of ample length and a thoughtful choice of fly. You're ready to move into casting position — almost! Another brief period of observation is important at this point — to secure a good foundation for the fly presentation. Firstly the fish should be located again — always a moment of relief. What are we looking for now? When you actually begin casting to the fish it will usually be from a different location from the spotting position. The new location will offer a new view, a new perspective. The trout may not be as easy to see or indeed not visible at all. Perception of angles and distances can change. So note the exact location of the trout with respect to in-river reference points or streamside points (rocks, vegetation, eddies, etc.). Note too the flow patterns of the river in the immediate vicinity and downstream of the trout (your assumed casting position). Are there variations in flow which may cause unwanted drag?

I fish, almost all of the time, with others at my side. I prefer it that way. The companionship is as much a part of the fun as catching the fish. No doubt a lot of anglers operate the same way. While two anglers together can enhance chances, particularly in less ideal conditions, we should be aware of the extra movement caused — another rod being waved about, different clothing, another pair of eager eyes equally keen to glimpse the fish and share the excitement. Two anglers — double your caution!

While it may appear I've suggested a painstakingly long and over-cautious approach, much of what I have said can in fact be achieved in a very short space of time. The leader could be prepared at the onset of fishing, the nymph already in use may suit the immediate situation. Observations of depth and feeding pattern may take only a few seconds.

So, while it is advised that riverbank movement be deliberate, discreet and preparations be exact, you should not dally. Some trout hold and feed in one position for hours, others may hold for only a few minutes then inexplicably patrol once downstream before returning and holding again, and others still, patrol continually. They're remarkably fickle these trout. Who knows what the next one will do?

Watch That Fish

From your observation point it may not be advisable to enter the river directly but, with rod low, head low, sure-footed, slowly, move downstream to a point where you know you're beyond the trout's detection — that's the point to enter the water (if entering the water is necessary) or the point from which you can move to your casting position. Proceed downstream, if you can, and try to keep your eye either on the fish or the exact river position where it was holding. This continued direct contact is extremely important, I feel. In fact,

*Observing a fish from a
concealed position.
Good technique.*

maintaining direct contact with the fish from the moment it is spotted
until it slips into the net is one of the foundations of success. Initially,
watching the fish helps with the observations mentioned before —
what it is feeding on, how deep it feeds, its feeding direction and so
on. But while making preparations (tying flies on, adjusting the leader,
adding an indicator), an occasional glance waterwards may glean more
important information and add fun by maintaining a high level of
excitement. One friend of mine, once he has spotted a fish, refuses
to face it because he gets too nervous and cannot concentrate on his
immediate tasks. Instead he always turns his back while making
preparations. I prefer (ever wary of flybox flash, etc) to allow
occasional reassuring glances waterwards, to look for more
information on the fish's movement and become more familiar with
the feeding habits and location.

As you move into your casting position it is a great advantage to keep the fish in view too. The advantage gained is a defensive one. While progressing upstream watch for the trout's movement. If it continues to feed regularly that's generally the time to make positive progress. But, fickle by nature, trout sometimes range beyond their feeding niches. Watch for this. Any downstream forays by the trout may prompt you to lower your body position, to lie on the bank (rod on the ground too) or even to retreat unobtrusively. All the time your objective is to keep a safe, undetected distance from the fish, while observing it, while making tackle preparations, while moving into casting position and while casting. All of this is only assured if you can see the fish.

If the trout is not visible while you are moving into casting position you are at a disadvantage but in that case you should try to watch, quite intently, the trout's supposed location. Why watch that spot? Well, as you move, change height, change direction, your perspective changes and, frequently, once the eyes have left the water, precise relocation can be difficult. While moving you can only assume the fish remains, maintaining previous habits. In all you do, err on the conservative, move with haste (but carefully), keep extra low, keep a safe distance away.

When two anglers are fishing together an unsighted fish (from water level) can be less of a problem. One angler can act as a spotter and relay movements to the other.

The Casting Position

Your immediate objective is to get into the most favourable casting position. But, what is the most favourable position? Opinion varies. Every situation is unique. Flow patterns need to be considered; overhead vegetation and river bank vegetation may obstruct. The relationship between casting arm and river bank being fished may be involved. Water depth may be a consideration. Where choice exists, I opt for a position downstream, usually directly behind the fish.

There are a number of good reasons for this decision. Firstly, the trout has one blind zone, out of its vision completely — and that is directly behind. By choosing a casting position adrift of the fish you are using this advantage. Secondly, from a rear position you can make one of three casts — to the fish's left (and drift fly or nymph down that side, nylon not over the fish), directly over the trout's head (and drift the fly really close) or to the fish's right (again avoiding putting line directly above).

Three important considerations will determine your choice. It may have been evident, while watching earlier, that the trout was taking most food out to its right. You would cast accordingly. It may be that the sun is to the fish's left, casting shadows from that direction. Again a cast to the right would be more sensible — line shadow would then not cross the fish. Drifts to one side then the other may not be heeded

Getting into a casting position behind a fish. Good technique

Casting to a trout's left

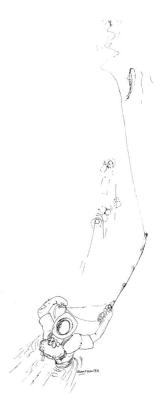

by the trout, but a drop directly ahead, bringing fly or nymph closer, may induce a take.

From a side-on or an oblique casting position the fly can still be drifted left, right or centre but drag-free drifts, without the dangers of mending line (see page??), are frequently shorter. To cast beyond a trout, that is to effect a drift on its far side, invariably puts tippet nylon (or more) over the fish while placing the floating line closer. In addition, from a side-on position an angler may be in or close to a trout's line of vision leaving fewer margins for error. Casting from a side-on position requires not only accuracy in direction but precision in length.

I feel there is a greater latitude from behind but there are some disadvantages. More often than not, the fish is more difficult to see from a low rear position and judging distances can be deceiving. Where there is variation in flow speed, some line mending may be necessary to avoid drag. To mend upstream may be more difficult from directly behind than from side-on.

Having a choice as to where to fish is a luxury. Often, overhead trees or vegetation behind determine not only where it is possible to cast from but also the type of cast you can use. Water depth or speed likewise may restrict choices even further.

Let's assume you are able to wade in behind and that is the choice you make. Do so with care. Avoid sending pressure waves upstream. The problems here are not great in fast, ripply water but in pools.

Check for casting hazards before putting a line in the air.

or zones of slower flow greater vigilance is necessary. Think too about crunching stones beneath your feet. Sound travels easily under water. Two stones or rocks grinding together emanate a strong signal. Beneath those stones is the habitat of numerous nymphs. A thought about possible habitat damage is not ridiculous either.

Trout possess an instinctive caution — an inherent natural mechanism for survival. So even the oft-scorned 30 centimetre trout is not always easy prey for an angler and will seek cover when alarmed. As trout grow so does their caution. Hence any fish beyond three kilograms, having survived a multitude of deceits, will not fall at all easily. The trout pictured on the cover of *Stalking Trout* is well beyond three kilograms. I'm often questioned about that photograph. The fish I imagine attracts the greatest interest. ''How big was it?'' ''Put up much of a fight?'' And somewhat veiled and falsely incidental

— "Where was it taken?" The first two are easily recalled, but my recollection fails me always on the third. It's written that every picture has a story — that one certainly has. The river name eludes me but every other detail remains vivid in my mind.

It could have been mine that fish, I spotted it. "Six pounds," I thought. "Ho's turn — I'll photograph the action."

Near the top it fed, towards the opposite bank — nymphs from just beneath the film and surface flies as they emerged. No flourish — the deliberation of a seasoned brown. Beneath lay the security of a bed beyond sight — 5-6 metres, merely a guess. Deep jade green. Heavily limbed beeches overhung the pool casting long shadows of a waning afternoon sun, cloaking us, the invaders, intruders with ill intent, compelled by the hunting urge. A cast was possible from an adjacent ledge. Not an easy one, a roll perhaps but certainly immediate. Not Ho's choice. A swift glance told him that near the far bank was wadeable. Only one limb overhead to negotiate and certainly clear well behind.

As he sought the best casting position I observed the fish. It displayed all the qualities of a trophy — vigilant, watchful, ponderous. Only momentarily did it hold in one position. Most of the time it moved, following a territorial path, not nosing the surface, but a metre down, maybe more. It eased towards the tail of the pool, skirted the shallower fringes but always over the verge of deep water. It would weave a path upstream, towards the stomach of the pool, in the tongue of stronger flow, then either turn and ease more deliberately downstream fringing the shallower edge or sometimes just allowing the gentle flow to push it backwards, drifting clear and visible in the sunlight or occasionally slipping unheralded through a long afternoon shadow only to emerge again further adrift.

Ho watched too as he waded the shallows at the tail of the pool then waited, moving upstream from shadow to shadow only when the fish moved up.

Casting a fly is easy. It has a rhythm, a flow, a pattern. Most anglers find it so — until that final drop is imminent. Then the back cast drops lower, tight loops widen and the fly climbs higher reaching for foliage above. I'm sure Ho remembers his first attempt here — the effortless initial style then the final thrust whistling into the only overhanging limb. The fish continued upstream, undaunted, unmolested.

Ho tugged the line. It broke leaving a metre of tippet, a reminder hanging loosely waterwards. Then he waded to the bank seeking the cover of shade and bush.

With a new tippet and fly came renewed hope. Ho dropped back into the water watching the fish constantly and maintaining a low profile, veiled in shadow.

That little thread of nylon, waving a gentle message, probably governed the next cast. It shot forward well beneath the limb, dispelled all power above the water and the fly drifted down lightly and naturally. Not quite where intended but it mattered little. The trout

Casting over the top of a trout.

23

reacted without delay. Up, up, up, it came. The snout appeared. The fly was gone. Ho hit hard. Which came first, the buckling rod or the whoop of success I cannot remember — maybe they were simultaneous. Into the depths dived the fish. Again it showed the character of a really large trout — nose down it hugged the bed, beyond sight, beyond control, immovable. A test of patience, deceivingly docile, yet still a six-pounder in our minds.

The end came with a flourish, before the fish was spent. After 20 minutes of skulking out of sight it inexplicably emerged at speed, into the shallows at the pool tail, then pounded through the rapids into the next pool. We chased, hopping from boulder to boulder, Ho with rod held high and me in pursuit, net ready. The pool below, churning turbulently, promised a violent fight and maybe it would have been. But into the foam and turmoil I dipped the net to await a later chance. Almost immediately, oblivious to my presence, the fish dived straight into the net. Only when I lifted did we realise the enormity of the fish. The length was there. Alone that's not enough. The depth was there. But so too was the shoulder width — broad and solid. A jackfish maybe, but clean, unblemished on either flank. No battle scars, no ragged fins — instead the freshness of youth.

Ho's success on that occasion was largely due to his care in selecting and reaching his casting position, his use of shadows, his preparations hidden by bush, his deliberate wading and constant visual contact with the fish — in all a sensitivity to the instinctive watchfulness, the constant vigilance of the trout.

2

Getting The Fly Into The Air

Last spring, I witnessed one of those magic moments of fishing. Unbelievable at the time, scoffed at in the retelling, undoubtedly never to be witnessed again. Yet true — an unforgettable personal treasure, more precious amid scepticism.

While a boisterous north-westerly swept the ranges, and increased the snowmelt, the major rivers of Canterbury ran high, unfishable. Further east though an early summer meant low clear streams.

It was a warm sunny day and, amid willow, swamp and pasture, insect life was abundant — damselflies, an occasional delicate mayfly, tiny moths and multitudes of unidentified creatures seeking refuge in the grasses or being buffeted across the stream. In the bright sun that rippling breeze was an angler's friend aiding in concealment and, with careful manoeuvring among the vegetation, assisting with casting too.

Loose line on the water — difficult to get into the air under control.

The stream John and I were fishing carried little water through ripply glides, over pebble beds, narrow and confined. But, like a number of Canterbury streams, this one opened occasionally into wide deep pools, willow-shaded and cool. Fringed with weed beds, fed from freestone runs, and with grassland all around, these pools provided ample food for trout.

The trout, without the luxury of a swift flow providing a regular food supply, actively sought their prey. Sometimes the depths or the security of shadow took them from sight but often, bold and obvious, they nosed amid weed, drifted just beneath the surface and even finned along muddy verges. All the time though their senses were divided — quick to discern food yet deceivingly alert to danger.

Our fishing technique, or more correctly John's this time, required patience, cunning and precision–patience in first watching the feeding pattern and waiting for an opportune moment to cast, cunning in remaining concealed, then precision in placing a fly accurately and delicately at an appropriate time. At John's left shoulder I observed, equally involved by just being there. Our position was perfect, cloaked in shade, fringed by tall shrubs yet with a convenient casting passage ahead to the water. We were aware of two fish feeding in the pool, one some distance away, never coming close. The second held our attention. A classic cruiser. It followed a regular path, appeared to take all offering from the bed beneath the surface and the floating morsels.

Three times it passed before John moved. He waited for it to fade from view then flicked his rod sharply up lifting several metres of line high,taking a small dry clear of menacing bush and grass. Forward once, up again, extending the line by a metre or two, then the second time forward and the fly was dropped, easily seen from the fish's previous feeding path. Moments later, breeze-assisted, any minor cast disturbance was gone. We sank a little lower and waited, waited the mandatory eternity, waited in silence, highly expectant. Eventually the trout eased into view then worked closer and closer to the fly. Right on path — five metres away, four, three. Closer and closer it got. About a metre short the nose should have lifted, tail tilted, in acknowledgment at least. Not so. A metre past, two metres past, three, four. We relaxed, disappointed but still hopeful.

"Next time," said John, "I'll drop the fly as it cruises along, add a little movement. That breeze-rippled surface should hide the cast."

The fish next appeared taking from the top, sip and dimple together. Again John employed only two deft flicks before willing the fly quietly down. The trout's response was immediate although unhurried. In moving towards the fly it lifted. I watched John's left hand, fingers entwining the loose line firmly, ready to tighten. The right hand tensed too, knuckles whitened. Right up to the fly weaved the trout, hesitated momentarily then continued below. Inspection completed but the mouth never opened. Again we relaxed.

"Maybe the fly wasn't sitting right," suggested John, "I'll give it another try." Two flicks of the rod. The fly drifted down. The fish inspected closely then continued as before, obviously unconvinced.

I'd have changed flies after the second refusal. John was tempted to do so but opted for third time lucky. The next drop brought the excitement. Just after the fly, twice rejected, had settled within the trout's vision, a delicate damselfly skimming centimetres above the water stopped and settled on our recently-placed platform. The trout's weaving ceased, its course straightened. Some distance from our friendly damselfly a gap appeared in the fish's jaws. Moments later, damselfly and imitation were engulfed as one. Only a lily white purist could have resisted striking then. Not John. The instant he hit, the trout erupted from the water. Skidding fully two metres sideways it then dived for cover, clearly alarmed yet eager to rectify its error. Despite one of the liveliest battles I've witnessed, the trout eventually succumbed to John's net. Whether from guilt about dubious deception or in the interests of conservation I did not ask, but John returned the fish quickly then turned to me, grinned and said, "Do you believe that?" I had no answer. I don't think there was one.

I've pondered on that incident often since. The vision of the damselfly landing, then the trout's eagerness to take remain foremost in my mind. But in hindsight I marvel at John's skill in quickly and precisely placing the fly exactly where he wished. There was no luck involved there but a number of quickly planned and executed manoeuvres. The first of them — getting the line into the air — forms the basis of this chapter.

A good tight line from hand to first stripping ring. A loose loop to reel. Good technique.

Common Problems

It is not my intention to offer a dissertation on the mechanics, dynamics or art of casting a fly. Others have already done that well and plenty of reference material is readily available. Instead I wish to focus on a few problems which Graeme and I have both observed as common to newcomers casting a fly or to more experienced anglers in moments of casual inattention.

The first stage in casting a fly or nymph is to get it into the air, an act fraught with problems for many beginners.

There are three golden rules which I feel could prove invaluable to all those anglers who find they frequently have to untangle knots or "birds' nests" in their leader or who find they often tangle line around rod, body and limbs:

Rule 1: Never begin the first lift until at least 1½ rod lengths of floating line have been stripped out of the tip ring of the rod.

Rule 2: Never try lifting your line into the air while the fly is close to your body and a lot of loose line lies between rod tip and fly.

Rule 3: When lifting the rod there should be a tight line from your free hand to the first stripping ring and loose line to the reel.

Failure with one or more of these points frequently besets most novices and leads to an inability to establish line control in casting — hence an unmolested fish.

Perhaps if we return to the position gained in Chapter One I could elaborate further.

Ahead, now almost within casting distance, a fish is feeding. It's still unaware of your presence or your intentions. In gaining your casting place you have sneaked upstream, rod low and out behind, parallel to the water surface. All the time, treading softly, you have been intent on watching the fish or concentrating on its feeding niche. Now you are ready to make preparations for casting.

For successful angling there are no short cuts. Fly fishing is an art and a science, a discipline. Failure to adhere to its code inevitably either alarms a fish or leads to an inability to place a fly near to one ripe for deception.

Casting A Nymph

Your preparations for casting — for first getting your nymph into the air under control — require, particularly for a novice, a methodical approach.

Let's assume your nymph is secured to a small hook ring just forward of the reel, that you have opted to fish from a downstream position and that you are standing in flowing water. Let's hope you are concentrating on that fish. Without doubt it's time for action. A step-by-step explanation may be easiest to follow at this point:

1. Keep the rod facing downstream.
2. Remove the hook from the hook ring.
3. Grip the rod in one hand above the handle (butt end towards the water and fish), high enough to allow the other hand to pull strips of line out through the tip ring.
4. Allow the nymph to float free downstream in the current.
5. Now strip the line out through the tip ring — the leader butt first followed by four to five metres of fly line.
6. Allow the current to drag all of this free downstream until the line is tight.

You are ready to cast. In compiling this list I have purposely simplified the procedure in two ways. Firstly I mentioned that you were using a nymph; secondly, the casting position was in running water. When fishing a nymph it is desirable to wet it prior to casting. Therefore it is an advantage to allow it to float freely in the current while you are stripping line. When the final cast is made it will immediately sink to its designed depth. By establishing a casting position in running water the current helps to carry nymph and line away from your body until the line straightens. This immediately provides a good basis for establishing good line control.

Casting A Dry Fly

But the procedure is not always as simple when it comes to dry fly fishing — considered by many to be the ultimate. It's certainly top of my list. For me seeing the trout's snout emerging to take, bold and visible, is exciting. In some ways, with the take obvious the strike is easier — or should be. But other facets make dry fly fishing more delicate, more precise, more difficult. Perhaps the difficulty adds to its mystique, its status.

In our present context of preparing to cast, stripping four to five metres of line from the rod tip is a little more complex because it must be done while keeping the dry fly off the water. So no longer can the tippet be allowed to drift freely downstream — otherwise the fly will be thoroughly dowsed prior to casting, sink when required to float and be rendered often ineffective. I can't emphasise this seemingly small point enough, mainly because it's a fault so commonly evident among new fly fishermen. Visual contact with the fish should be paramount all the time, so too should be following your dry fly on the water. This is only possible if it floats well, high and clear.

To strip line from rod tip and effectively keep the dry fly dry I work as follows:

Firstly I remove the fly from the hook ring in my left hand then lift my rod tip high with my right hand pulling down with my left. This removes most of the leader. Then, with the fly still held in my left hand I reach up and strip the floating line with the free fingers, letting it fall free. The fly remains held. Then another strip is effected. I drop the fly only when sufficient line is free of the rod tip to begin casting efficiently. All this is easier with my shorter (2.3 metre) rod. With a 2.7 metre rod my right hand usually grips near the first stripping guide as suggested earlier.

Why labour the point of stripping four to five metres of line free of your fly rod prior to lifting? I stress the point because failure to do so is a source of so much frustration among novice fishermen. To cast a fly effectively an angler relies on two things — the life and power of his rod and the weight of his line. Both are required to work together.

Line straight down stream — easier to get into the air under control.

So often I see fishermen beginning their casting with the leader only extending from the rod tip. As they strip from their reel and power forward and back, the floating line shoots out in an increasing bow between the two tip rings. Others strip line from the reel and can't manage to extend it past the first guide. Meanwhile the tippet, out of control, develops wind knots, wraps around the rod tip or, worse still, embeds itself somewhere unwanted. The only way to get fly or nymph into the air, under control, is to have rod and line working as one. The line requires the power of the rod. The rod requires line weight, not the tippet alone or just a metre of line, to work with.

The amount of line required to get started varies. My 4-5 metres is a safe general figure. With a short rod, (less than 2.4 metres) the line length will be less than with a longer rod. Similarly the optimum casting line will differ with rod length. Short rods are more efficient with short lines.

I'm a little uneasy when it comes to criticising novice casters and pointing out their failings in getting their line under initial control. Such comments are tinged with hypocrisy. Place a freely feeding brown trout a short distance from me and I often wrap loops of line around the rod tip, entangle my reel, impale my fly in clothing and so on — usually as a result of excessive haste. It still happens regularly, fortunately usually unseen. But one horrifying time remains on record — if my friends have their way — for ever.

Alan Pannett and I were interested in making a video about the upstream approach to fly fishing. For several weeks we engaged in a punctuated fishing style — stalking upstream to find a feeding fish then setting up portable video gear, positioning it where terrain allowed, to capture as much action as possible. One location I remember well. A fine trout fed freely, in a ripply run, ranging wide to both sides in less than a metre of water. The stream was bathed in sun, ideal for ''filming'', while a backdrop of dark shaded beeches added ideal contrast.

With recorder ready to run, camera set, we were prepared to go, Alan on camera, me with rod. The stalk was faked, a careful upstream stalk, an over-acted sighting, head bobbing, eye shading, body lowering all textbook style yet grossly overdone. But from there on the acting ceased. The camera was forgotten and my nervous approach to the fish began. As I crept in behind the fish, perhaps 15 metres downstream of it, I began preparing to cast. The five metres of leader were removed from my rod followed by just two metres of floating line. In my haste, concentrating intently on the fish, I attempted half-heartedly to lift the line into the air. I flicked it weakly forward then equally poorly back. The forward roll wrapped one loop of line around the rod tip, the backcast added a second. The camera watched.

That was just the beginning. Aware of my poor attempt to get the line into the air and of the impending danger, I should have stopped there, accepted the error and undone the tangle methodically. Instead

I opted to ''de-loop'' the hard way. What I tried to do was reverse the tangle with reverse flicks of the rod tip. The result — a mass of nylon and fly line closely matted, a tangle taking ten seconds to manufacture and ten minutes to remedy.

My nymph had not yet tempted the fish. The recorder rolled on, capturing all, telling no lies. Fortunately, in making the final video we were able to edit out most of the errors and highlight the excitement. Those who have viewed the edited product since probably missed the initial moments of tangle formation uncut, action essential to the continuity of the ''film'', but I see it plainly and cringe — a harsh reminder of the care needed to load a fly rod with sufficient fly line prior to lifting, the first act in casting a fly.

Line Control

Now to the second major source of problems faced by budding fly fishers. I can write about it with confidence as I still offend in the area of line control. Stated simply, too frequently we endeavour to lift the fly off the water while it lies somewhere close to our feet. In other words, what we are trying to do is lift nine plus metres of line (five metres of fly line and four of leader) from a loosely coiled repose to an immediate taut control. If we don't get if right the results can include flies embedded in breeches and sleeves, nymphs wrapping themselves around rods, streamside vegetation snagged immediately (particularly behind) or, most devious of all, the hook tip unwittingly and deftly removed on a bouldery bank.

A roll cast to get fly and line airborne and get fly away from body.

Getting ready to roll cast.

Good fly casting means line control. A line under control is a tight line, not only in initiating the first cast but right up to netting a fish. A tight line should aid the first back cast. It is the basis of false casting, and controls the fly drop. While the fly or nymph drifts towards a fisherman close contact between fly and hands must be maintained by stripping. A strike can only be effected with an ability to tighten immediately while firm control forms the basis of all landing strategies.

How then can we establish a tight line prior to lifting it into the air? The method I employ most frequently is a simple forward roll cast. It need not be a perfect or complete roll with line and fly laid delicately or fully extended, usually it isn't. But what I aim to do is, by sharply powering the rod tip forwards and waterwards (from about 12 o'clock) roll or flick the floating line away from my body. From a more distant position a tight line is established by the time the rod has reached 10 o'clock in the first back cast, hence there is still plenty of rod action and rod power left (10 o'clock to 1 o'clock) to establish fast line speed. I use this roll cast method when I first start fishing and I also use it while actively pursuing an upstream trout. Often, after my fly or nymph, unheeded by fish, has drifted, it floats menacingly closer to me. Prior to lifting I roll it upstream again (short of the fish!) then power into the next back cast.

A second method for establishing a tight line prior to the initial lift is even more simple. It merely uses the flow of a stream to do the job. An angler preparing to cast to a fish upstream (particularly if he is waterbound) need only drop the line from the rod tip into the flow and allow the current to carry all downstream until the line is tight. The initial cast here, the lift into the air, is in fact a forward cast, but one more likely to form a basis for early line control because the fly has lifted some distance from the angler's body. This procedure can also be employed while actively pursuing a fish. When the fly, rejected as it often is, has passed the fish it can then be allowed to drift past the angler too and continue downstream until line and leader straighten in the flow.

It seems almost totally wrong for me to separate elements of casting like lifting the line from the water, control in the air and so on. All are part of one flowing, total action. Rod and line work together, respond to arm and wrist, reflect every command obediently. Then there's the non-casting hand — all the while playing a vital role in maintaining a tight line (or contact between angler and fly so that a tight line can easily and efficiently be established) whether you are about to strike a fish or initiate the next hope-filled cast.

The Non-Casting Hand

The non-casting hand, for many new fly fishers, is a forgotten aid. Here is a further problem in co-ordination likely to beset the would-be caster. But the non-casting hand plays a vital role in fish catching, one underestimated by many. Concentration is on the casting arm and the other arm clutches the line uncertainly, behaving itself at times, but often fumbling.

It is essential that the non-casting hand never be allowed to let go of the line. Allow it to slip freely on occasions, yes — but never let it go. The only time there should be tight line between hand and reel is when stripping line from the reel to add to casting distance. At all other times the hand should act as a link, between a tight line to the first stripping guide and the loose line between hand and reel.

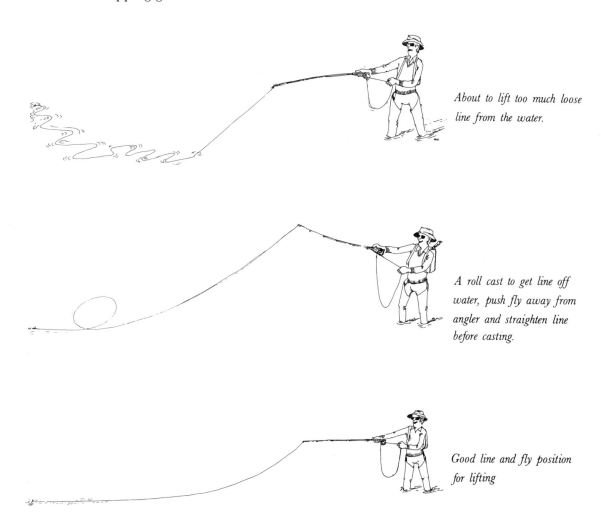

About to lift too much loose line from the water.

A roll cast to get line off water, push fly away from angler and straighten line before casting.

Good line and fly position for lifting

Beginning The Cast

Back now to getting the fly into the air. I observe two major faults commonly displayed by anglers in initiating a cast. Let's assume the casting arm is the right arm. In beginning a cast, that is in lifting

Beginning with a good length of floating line.

the line into the air, the right forearm lifts powerfully back and up. Thus power is imparted to the rod and in turn to the line. The goal is to transfer the power into high line speed. Proper use of the non-casting hand can add both to the balance of the lift and to the line speed.

Again the action should be all as one. As the right arm is tensed in readiness for the backcast (or should it be termed an upcast?), the left hand should grasp the line firmly near the first stripping guide. As the right arm powers back and up, the non-casting hand should pull equally sharply down — technically known as a single haul. The conclusion of the backcast should show a tight, straight line from fly to rod tip — tight line through the rod guides (or rings), tight line from first stripping guide to left hand and finally a loose length of line hanging between left hand and reel. The two hands should be a distance apart, the length of the fish you'd like to catch!

A single haul not only increases line speed in the air but diminishes the length of line in the air. Therefore control is easier. Rarely during a casting action should there be loose line between the left hand and the stripping guide. Yet here is a common source of error. Too frequently all the line tightening, line speed, line control is left to the casting arm. The left hand, at the best, does nothing more than hold the line.

Often too I see the left hand, correctly clutching the line, but wrongly following the right hand up — the line tight between first guide and hand and between hand and reel. Left hand line control here is virtually non-existent. Equally commonly the left hand can be seen to exert equal pull to the first stripping guide and to the reel extracting some line from each. This can be a fatal error. Firstly it diminishes the effectiveness of the left hand in line control and secondly, stripping more line from the reel may result in too much line being cast and a fish being alarmed. Harsh words maybe but they are born from common observation of novices and continual personal analysis. While self-improvement requires some clinical, serious evaluation and plenty of ongoing practice, one should retain a sense of reality, not become too indulgent and retain a sense of humour. What happens in the books does not always follow on the river.

It's rare for me to fish alone, one day in 20 may be an exaggeration. One of those rare outings took me to the Mataura River 50 kilometres from my Invercargill home. The place, rural to the water's edge, cropped to flood lines, had become very familiar over 20 or more years. I no longer needed to stop to gain access, my car was known.

· Being Southland, bracing in the spring, waders were a necessity. These were extracted from the car boot and donned. Next came a warm jacket and a well-secured hat. Clothed snugly, it was time to prepare my rod. Not in the boot. It never is. Nor in the car. Had I wife or child they could have been blamed for my omission. Were there a companion the finger could have been pointed his way. There were no avenues of scorn beyond personal stupidity.

Beginning with the fly away from the body and rod.

I'd driven 50 kilometres to go fishing. An inherent Irish stubbornness deemed it would be so — but how? A distant conversation with the farmer sprang to mind — he'd trodden the river banks on occasion, ignoring sheep, seeking trout instead. Perhaps, with the promise of a trout, he'd lend me a rod.

Somewhat hesitantly, I approached the farmhouse, where the farmer's wife, who answered my call, was more amused by the situation than I, although I tried to share the mirth. She said there was a fly rod somewhere in one of the wool sheds. I followed her there. A fly rod indeed, extracted from a high shelf, trailing ancient spider silk as it was handed down. The reel was there tightly secured with line still threaded and lure attached. Lure? On the Mataura, mecca

A roll off the water to push the fly away from the body.

35

for the dry fly? Not the time to mention that. It was not until I had returned to the river that I fully appreciated the character of the rod I'd borrowed. Had I been more observant perhaps I'd have been less bold in promising a trout. How many guides should a rod possess? Seven at least? My 2.7-metre rod has eleven. This one had four. Four would not have been quite so bad were they better placed — the tip ring was there, but what a menacing distance to the next guide down. Three close together, then no more.

I was glad at that point that I was alone. To have a witness to my initial casting attempts would have dented my pride. Those that followed were little better. On forward strokes line shot out in three places — a huge loop low down, a sizable loop before the tip guide and a little more beyond that. As the morning wore on a whole new set of casting rules were written and eventually some line extension was achieved.

It's rare for me to catch ten trout in a day. Pristine rods, newly dressed lines, well oiled reels, finely tuned techniques don't seem to add to ten. But, with that battered gear that day, I achieved the magic number.

It was a bolder angler who returned to the farmhouse. Two fine trout accompanied the highly acclaimed rod into a thankful pair of hands. At that point I noticed a fine thread hanging from just below the tip ring. My eye followed it up then rolled around where it was meant to be held. Binding silk, almost unravelled. I could visualise then, the next user an hour into his day, devising as I had just done, some new strategies for getting the fly into the air.

3

Control In The Air

In all sports there seem to be plenty of over-proud participants who need to twist the truth to bolster their performances. Few fishermen are not so afflicted to some degree. Unseen trout, lost or returned, assume fine proportions. "The other day," was always one to remember. "You should've been there," and so on. Often the exaggeration becomes a truth for the teller and is rarely challenged. Open disbelief, after all, can only cast doubt on one's own tales!

Occasionally though one can get an insight into the magnitude of the fabrication.

Good fast line speed.

Several seasons ago I camped with some friends on the banks of a very famous Southland stream. In the evening, as the sun (golden to the end in a crisp, clear sky) faded below the horizon we moved streamwards to await an evening rise. The conditions exuded promise. No wind, birds dipping waterwards, insect life awakening.

The three of us each sought solitude. I reclined where I could survey the whole of my chosen pool. Upstream a bouldery "ripple" promised a nursery for mayfly nymphs and an abundance of caddis hopefully readying themselves to leave their watery home, to seek their ultimate goal — adulthood and procreation in the air. The bank opposite, lined with willows, offered a welcome backdrop, excluding unwelcome glare, a hindrance to observing hints of waxing activity. The trees too housed other unseen observers. Two swallows emerged then dived suddenly, expertly, snatching insects beyond my sight.

Bird activity can be a great help to observant fishermen — on sea or river alike. They act, not as catalysts, but as infinitely observant respondents, more acutely tuned to nature's delicate transitions. More dependent, thus keener than us. Their activity here lifted my senses.

Downstream the first rise appeared, more of a slash than a dimple. The rise form suggested a small fish — the flourish, the haste of youth. "Wait longer," I thought. "Wait for the parents to join the feast — maybe Grandad!" I waited.

Before long there were more surface disturbances — not just in the tail of the pool now, but mid-pool and, a little later, towards the head, the prime spot, the place of dominant trout. Convinced the time was right I sneaked waterwards, mid-pool, above where I assumed the little ones played, right where the unhurried sipping suggested real fish.

And so it was. Only one drift of a tiny Dad's Favourite was necessary. Close to the far bank it rode then disappeared from view amid a diminutive dimple. I struck firmly. The fish dived, then hastened downstream. Seemingly satisfied that all its offspring were

The result of poor line control.

given warning of my intrusion, my ever-growing fish quickly turned only to disturb the upper population of the pool too. Had I landed the fish I may have felt some justice had been served but alas one energetic leap induced an excessively tight line and hook and flesh parted company. When the wake of that final flourish subsided, a calm pervaded the water's surface. The insects emerged in abundance. The birds fed on. The fish, vigilantly patient, awaited my departure.

Depart I did — earlier than I had hoped. On my way campwards I passed the second of our party. He stood mid-stream, knee-deep, flicking back and forth, oblivious to my presence. From my distant position I could not distinguish the rising fish being tempted. It was clear though that one in particular held focus. Each successive cast probed the same vicinity. It was clear too that the fish lay some distance ahead — a long line of at least 20 metres curled forward then back repeatedly. To keep 20 metres of line airborne, under control, is no mean feat. In this instance it was reaching its goal with power but, at the same time, occasional back casts dropped low, flicking the water behind and even at times resting the fly momentarily. I'm sure of that because, to the angler's dismay, and to my amusement, one thrust forward met quite unexpected resistance from behind. The forward cast did not become airborne. A very quick trout, one of those youthful slashers, seized the fly on its backcast. When the angler had fully realised his plight, had turned and commenced to reel in the captive I emerged onto the scene.

"Got one, I see," I offered.

"Not too big," was the reply.

"Was it far out?" I asked.

"Midstream."

"Fussy?"

"Not this one."

I probed no further, and did not reveal I'd been watching for some time. To be fair the truth was admitted after a generous nightcap.

Who could resist? A really unique deception, a quite unusual event versus a common error in casting, a small lapse in control in the air. A fish on your back cast — that takes some beating.

The Back Cast

This brings me to the point I would like to stress most strongly in this chapter — the back cast should not drop below the horizontal which presupposes that the rod should not drift back to much beyond 1 o'clock. I stress this because, in my observation, this is the most common error displayed by newcomers to fly fishing, leading to their inability to power their fly much beyond their leader on the water.

The common scenario looks like this. The angler stands knee-deep in water. The rod is lifted quickly then back. The line follows, flicking the water behind. On the forward cast the rod stops at 10 o'clock then back it goes to 3, forward to 10, back to 3. The next cast is intended to be the one lowered to the water. The back cast drops lower, a subconscious effort to achieve more power, then the forward cast loses its power much too early. The forward stroke thrusts the floating line forward but all power dissipates too soon and the leader drops vertically in a heap a metre ahead of the floating line. The angler's inclinations number two:

1. To shuffle forward a little with his feet.
2. To strip more floating line from the reel.

Both are incorrect decisions. "So," you may say, "that's the common problem. So what's the common answer?"

I'll attempt to explain, again, as in Chapter Two, by trying to adhere to the specific errors I've seen newcomers commonly make rather than give you a detailed description of casting.

Let's take "one pace backwards" and briefly establish our progress in Chapter Two. There the difficulty was one of successfully getting the fly into the air. The basis for success, it was suggested lay in three manoeuvres:

1. Begin to cast with at least a rod length of floating line or more.
2. Begin casting only when the fly is well away from the body.
3. Haul on the fly line with the non-casting hand as an equal part of the casting act.

Correct rod stop — high at one o'clock — high back cast.

These things done we got to the point where our line was in the air, mobile. Our concern now is to establish control of that line in the air then use it as a sound foundation for a delicate, governed placement of fly or nymph, where intended, as intended.

Lifting The Fly

When lifting the fly into the air for the first time, try to get your line moving at a very fast speed. The lift should be performed using the whole forearm and all its power. Begin the lift gently, lifting the line gradually from the water, thus reducing friction — the water's grip — then increase the power, snapping the wrist and forearm upwards. The wrist should not snap right back — otherwise the rod will follow — but the action should stop with your thumb pointing skywards. This wrist action is a subtle one — not in the power it imparts but in the magnitude of movement. Think of the action as an up cast rather than a back cast. Think of propelling the fly skywards rather than backwards. The power stroke of the rod should be only in the vicinity of 100 degrees so, on the up cast your rod should stop at 1 o'clock. Stop it dead. Don't allow it to drift back further. Then wait until the line has straightened completely behind. Then, equally powerfully, work the forearm forwards. As previously keep the wrist almost locked with the forearm pushing all the time on the forward stroke with your thumb.

Three Common Foibles

In this short summary of a precise, fundamental action, I've hinted at three foibles common to would-be casters. Overcome these and success will be closer.

Rod too far back for good line control.

Line control with left hand.

Firstly, too frequently the fly line and fly are not propelled at high speed. Instead of the line travelling backwards in a tight loop and straightening emphatically it moves in a wide arc, never really straightens at all but instead arcs loosely backwards then groundwards. The same sort of path can too often be observed in front. High line speed is essential for control. It's the foundation of control. Without it there's no real straightening, there's no precision, no base to build on.

The second common discrepancy, and probably the most fundamental and universal, is the habit of taking the rod too far back. By this, I mean, habitually the rod stops, not at 1 o'clock, not at 2 o'clock, but back parallel to the ground. If the rod goes back that far then the line will go at least that low but usually much lower. The results are too familiar — flies lost, lines broken, barbs broken. These are bad enough but less clear, and far more frustrating to the beginner, is the loss of power where it is required on the forward drive. There's often power upwards but it is not sustainable and certainly insufficient to drive the fly several metres beyond the fly line and deliver it to the water in that position. Without the power being directed in the right place we cannot satisfactorily achieve our goal of line control. What we should endeavour to do is to have our line straightening high in the air behind. This can be achieved in two ways:

First, thinking of the cast behind as an up cast, stop the upward power abruptly at or close to the upright. If the rod is stopped at 12 o'clock the line will shoot skywards. If it is stopped at 1 o'clock the line will be propelled back a little lower but still upwards. A stop at 2 o'clock will see the line heading back close to horizontally (assuming there is enough power and line speed). Thus it can be seen that the stopping position of the rod tip will determine the height

41

of the back cast (or up cast if executed correctly). A second aid to keeping a high line behind, and particularly when obstructions threaten behind, is to lift the elbow in the up cast.

For the angler who has difficulty in overcoming the problem of dropping his rod too low behind there is a little tip I once read which is worth a try. For a righthanded caster the natural comfortable stance in casting is with the left foot marginally ahead. This is particularly so while practising and watching the line behind. Try altering this so that the right foot is the one ahead. From this position it is more difficult to drop the back cast.

The third common error lies in the timing of the power strokes of the rod. In describing the back stroke I tried to emphasise the pausing to allow the line and leader to straighten. So often this is not done. Instead the forward stroke is begun while the reverse loop is still uncurling, with the result that the tippet may crack like a whip, dislodging the fly completely or in a short time dismantling the fly tier's painstaking work. Again it's the subtle outcome which is ultimately the most crucial. To err by not delaying the forward stroke until the back cast has straightened results in loss of part of the forward power, the casting power being used up as the fly turns. Thus the fly does not get delivered where intended.

Back And Forth

It must be a puzzling sight for a non-fisherman watching a fly angler practising his or her art. It must appear, with all of the airborne activity — back, forward, back, forward — that the angler spends far more time with the fly distantly tempting fish rather than its being intimately available to them. I wonder too if newcomers really question what this flicking back and forth repeatedly is all about. A little understanding of this may help solve some of the problems which develop in it.

A fly fisherman propels his fly skywards for a number of reasons:
1. It has completed its drift on the stream and needs to be replaced for a further try.
2. It may be the first cast towards a fish or promising spot.
3. As part of replacing the fly and part of the air control may be a change in direction which could require several backward-forward motions.
4. If fishing dry fly, time in the air at high speed helps remove water from the fly and adds to buoyancy.
5. In the backward-forward actions greater line length can be achieved through action with the left hand: (a) being stripped from the reel during a backstroke or (b) being released forward during a forward drive.

Whether the reason for keeping or putting the fly airborne be one or all of these I work to a golden rule. As long as my fly is not on the water there is no chance of catching a trout — no chance at all. In other words the more time my fly is on the water the greater my chance of inducing a take. Hence I try to keep airborne activity to a minimum. I try to work to the pattern of establishing control in the air as quickly as possible — a roll in front, a back cast, then the forward drop. Fishing dry fly I may add one more false case to remove more water. Fishing a nymph I'll often use just a back cast then drop the nymph on the first motion forward. In the right circumstances there won't even be a back cast, just a forward roll.

Good line speed with tight loop.

Good line straightening on forward false cast. Ready to back cast again.

Good use of left hand. Tight line to first stripping guide with loose loop to the reel.

Too often I watch new fly fishers keeping their fly or nymph airborne for innumerable false casts for no apparent reason apart from the observation that that's what fishermen do. The result is more chance for wind knots, more chance for tangles, more chance to lose control and less chance to tempt a fish.

During this airborne vigil another source of error may be apparent. In their quest for line control, anglers become aware that greater line speed is necessary. So, the rod action speeds up — forward, back, forward, back, in quick succession. The action accelerates, but the rod power remains the same. The result is less line control, not more. Watch the wrist action at this time too. A fast whippy rod action and excessive wrist use may seem a consistent combination, but wrist movement throughout the casting action should be very small. The wrist should not be the pivot of the casting action. The pivot should be the elbow. During an up cast the elbow should move a little backward and marginally upward, reversing the path on the forward power. By using the whole forearm the fast, whippy action and excessive wrist use should be avoided.

A pupil of mine, Anton Frayle, availed me with a success story last season. Anton showed an interest in learning to fish with a fly early in the year — but, more importantly, he displayed, in his enthusiasm, an unusual willingness to listen, assimilate and, above all, the discipline to practise.

The first advice he heeded was to purchase wisely. Not an excessively expensive rod but one combining strength, power and lightness — suitable for a 13-year-old boy and not too demanding on his pocket. Carbon? Yes, and a light, cheaper reel to balance.

Next came the initial attempts to cast. I doubt that Anton had any more than an hour of one-to-one tuition in total. The teaching sessions lasted no more than five minutes, then I instructed him to practise

Line straightening in front with false cast.

44

Line straightening behind with back cast.

daily for about ten to fifteen minutes. First I got him just lifting the fly into the air once, then putting it down. After a few days' practice the next session aimed at adding air control to this lifting process. And so we proceeded. Five minutes' tuition — several days' practice. Anton did not fail in his homework. Hence by the time a real opportunity to fish arose I had little doubt about a positive outcome.

The best time to point a newcomer fishwards is early in the season. There seem to be greater trout numbers then and their feeding seems more avid. Spring rains need to be endured but the real enthusiast barely notices.

The spring of 1988 will be remembered on the West Coast of the South Island. Equinoxal rain dropped incessantly for a seemingly eternal period. Between showers, pupil and teacher ventured waterwards — one stepping into the unknown, eager, willing, hopeful, but above all practised. The other watchful, wary, methodical, but with a hand secretly pocketed, two fingers crossed.

Our river, swollen and menacing, reputedly held low fish numbers so our quest was confined to the very edges. The first 400 metres revealed nothing and the next 100 metres of rapid held little hope. Then a more placid stony edge slowed us down and offered a hint of success. The river bed material, by the nature of its size and a shade of algae cover, suggested some stability and perhaps a breeding ground for caddis and mayflies. Intuition prevailed — a sizable brown performed its early season dance, a step left, return, a step right, return. I couldn't say that Anton hustled into casting position — he heeded the warning for care — but somehow he stood 15 metres downstream of the fish within moments. His hours of training became suddenly worthwhile. His nymph, successfully airborne, was soon propelled by sufficient line. It was dropped. It was taken. The fight

45

was on. The fish played fastidiously to the water's edge rolled onto its side. Momentarily the line lay slack and the nymph dropped from a gaping jaw. Immobilised, we stood watching the fish, surprisingly unhurried, snake away. I felt we'd been successful — a fish had been fooled, hooked, the job had been done. Anton seemed to accept that. His first fish. Proudly he told his father when we met for lunch.

In the early afternoon our upstream search continued. This time on a braided channel, a side stream clearly more stable and backed by a substantial bank bound with forest to the edge. One of the pleasant things about braided channels is their resemblance to a small stream. This one supposedly escaped the brunt of spring freshes because we soon found the fish were more plentiful. The first, I'm certain, will remain most clearly in Anton's mind. It was hooked, played and landed. Again Anton claimed a first to his Dad — but this time with unbridled enthusiasm and utmost conviction.

The story does not end there. So competent was Anton, as the result of his hours of grass-bound practice, that he could repeatedly lay a fly in a fish's path without causing alarm. In addition he was able to direct the fly left or right as required. All this skill was needed on the next fish. It fed in a shallow, ripply edge, intercepting surface flies or ranging wide to nymphs. A Dad's Favourite, riding high, realistically to us, gained close inspection for several metres downstream. A second dry, Kakahi Queen I think, was acknowledged too as was a small pheasant tail nymph. I think I enjoyed the contest more than Anton. To encounter fickleness added new dimensions to the lessons while renewed hope with each fly change buoyed expectation to greater heights.

A good tight loop.

Another nymph, again rejected. A further dry, same fate. As time passed calculation dwindled to possibilities then guesswork and waning faith. We'd not quite reached despair when, uncharacteristically, an inspection did not cease five centimetres from the fly. Instead the snout emerged and engulfed it — a size 14 sedge.

At this point I had to applaud my pupil. All of us so-called experienced anglers know only too well how often we've struck prematurely at an unexpected take. Anton, on his third strike ever, waited, as instructed, then met his just reward — the thrill of solid resistance succeeded by an arm-wrenching dash midstream.

Regular Practice

The foundation of an unforgettable first day on the river for Anton lay in his willingness to practise. Not sessions of great duration but frequent — almost daily — spells of ten to fifteen minutes. The regularity is paramount, the briefness important. In a short space of time, hand, wrist, forearm, shoulder and brain all get time to co-ordinate, and the brain is able to compute and assimilate. Meanwhile the arm tires little, not enough for success to diminish unacceptably. Strength soon grows.

I've heard some claims that an angler can be taught to cast in one spell of a few hours. I have grave reservations. A hunter can be taught to fire a rifle in a matter of hours too. But firing a gun and succeeding with game are two surprisingly different matters. So too is casting a fly and performing the same act with a fish ahead. To achieve consistent success means a commitment to regular practice. Not on the river — that's for fishing — but on the lawn or better still on a pond.

Unfortunately ponds do not exist close to many budding anglers' homes. The alternative is the lawn. Concrete or other forms of paving offer a smoother surface along driveways, footpaths and so on but I suspect they would fatally damage a floating line. For that reason I've discouraged the people I've taught to use such areas.

Long grass, meaning uncut lawns, is not ideal either. The upright and slightly curved blades cling to the line leading to an excessively false lift. Mown grass, however, allows a line to lie freely on top and offers similar resistance to water during an initial lift.

While practising on the lawn it's often very helpful to employ a marginally different stance. Instead of the feet being side by side (or close to it) pull the right foot back even further (this assumes you are a right-handed caster). This new stance swivels the body around slightly allowing easy visibility to the front and behind.

The vision behind is important. During practice the need to pinpoint a trout ahead does not exist. The focus of attention at this time is on what is happening to the line, and its extremity in particular. Some results can be gauged by feel, even by sound, but the best form of self-evaluation is to combine these with sight. What I'm suggesting is that when practising there's much to be gained by watching both the forward cast and the back cast. Too often anglers observe the former but never look behind. The consequence is a poor back cast. While watching the back cast you should look for line speed, the shape of the loop and whether or not the line is straightening before being driven forward.

Also watch the rod tip. How much below 1 o'clock does it drop? If you observe the rod tip stopping high, the line being driven high and quickly up in a tight U to straighten above horizontal then your action deserves applause. If, however, you see a great arching U which is never able to straighten before falling then there's a need for more power, more line speed. Self-analysis is an essential part of all learning. When analysing your own casting, frequent observation of the back cast, is paramount.

I'm not only a believer in self-analysis but also in using correct techniques during practice. Repeated faults soon establish themselves as habit and soon manifest themselves on the river. One technique which can be practised and established as a reflex is the correct use of the non-casting hand — in most instances the left hand. Too often I observe this as a mere line holder which grips the line tightly as the other hand lifts the rod backwards. The result is equal line tension between hand and first guide and hand and reel. Often during this power action a little more line clicks off the reel. Thus in three or four false casts the little bits add up — maybe to as much as a metre. In practice try to maintain tension to the first ring (stripping guide) only. Have a loop of line reelwards.

Although I've never measured I would say that I fish to the majority of my trout from a range of 8 to 13 metres. If this is so, then there's no need to practise casting with a longer line. Practising and fishing with an excessively long line is a frequent mistake. Twenty metres of straight line may look impressive but few have the skills to execute the manoeuvre — fewer still with a trout ahead. Our objective is to impress the trout not the onlookers. In most instances 12 metres of line will achieve your aim admirably.

4

Putting The Fly Down

As the curtain of winter comes down the fishing season and the void of home-bound months looms close. Real enthusiasts still snatch some enjoyable hours on the river. The last day of April 1989 I spent on my favourite stream, not with high expectation but certainly hoping for a mid-afternoon mayfly hatch and a brief duration of feeding activity.

Stopping rod just above horizontal when dropping fly.

Each month of a fishing season, I'm learning, has a subtly different feel and aura. From changeable Octobers of shower and squall to balmy mid-summer evenings and sparkling clear streams, and then the yellows and browns of autumn. Viewing continually through a camera it's the light I notice most, and the April sun is among the best. At this time the sun swings lower than at any other part of the fishing season. The sparkle of summer transforms to a resplendent sheen midstream while through long shadows a myriad of colours signals life's gradual slumber.

April 30 is deep into autumn. Engulfed by shadow I trod a bank possessing a peculiar mix of willow and beech — the willow gifting colour, the beech heralding the fringes of a wilderness area. From the trees I emerged onto a narrow well-grassed terrace giving a perfect view of the river three metres below. Rod concealed behind, I gently parted the grasses and peered into the depths. I was immediately grateful for instinctive caution and slow gradual movements, because directly below, a rod length away, a fine brown fed — not in the depths but right on top, enjoying an accumulating feast swept into its backwater territory. At that moment I was powerless to act, the fish was so near. I just watched, enjoying the detail afforded by my proximity. My only regret, in retrospect, lay in not observing details of the feeding. Instead I was preoccupied with the possibilities of deception and capture.

It was immediately clear that the fish had to move away before any attempts could be made. And there were other problems. Directly overhead and behind hung huge beech trees. All around me were tall grasses — brown, dried and seed-laden. A back cast was beyond reason. The more I looked, left and right, a roll cast seemed an impossibility too. What now? How could I get my fly onto the water? Somewhere from the depths of my mind I recalled a cast devised just for this situation. I'd read about it years ago and, coincidentally, had recently been talking about its use on willow-bound Canterbury streams. I'd never tried it, hadn't even practised it. Maybe I'd even scoffed at it. Yet before me it seemed the only way — the ultimate test. The fish's feeding path passed so close I had the "freedom" to

Poor technique for putting the fly down. The angler has let the line go with left hand and is leaning too far forward.

cast no more than two metres of line, meaning less than half of my leader only — no floating line.

The trick I'd been told, was called ''The Bow and Arrow'' cast. It entailed gripping fly or nymph tightly between thumb and forefinger then pulling back, flexing the rod in a taut backward arc. Pushing on the rod butt with the other hand apparently helped gain tension too. Below the fish eased up the back water, opening its ample jaws to suspended nymphs and sipping spent insects from above.

For a short time I lost contact. The fish fed beyond sight. In those moments I elected to practise the assault. Certainly an inappropriate occasion for trial, not what I'd dictate for a scholar, but immediate regrets had to be cast aside. I gripped the nymph, pulled back cautiously (aware of the closeness of thumb and hook) then ''twang''. The rod tip shot forward followed immediately by the nymph dropper and dry fly. But I'd obviously underestimated the power required. Fly, nymph and nylon all dropped harmlessly in a heap — not extended as hoped. Another thing I found in that very important first attempt was that my rod sprang perilously closely to the water. To catapult the tip into the water with a fish nearby would mean immediate disaster. The fish was still beyond sight. I tried once more. This time I worked the rod much harder and endeavoured to stop it sooner, higher above the water. The result proved infinitely more effective extending line ''well beyond'' the rod tip.

A gentle bankward flow and surface chop soon pushed my fly right to the water's edge, not where I wanted it. I had no choice but to wait, nymph in hand, and delay the cast until the fish fed closer.

I can recall the next moments quite vividly. The fish hesitated right on the surface, rolling lazily with the chop. I think perhaps it should have seen my rod tip spring out of the grass. Maybe it did but it became immediately more interested in the tiny plop of my nymph a metre ahead. One sideways flick of its tail and a backwards push with pectoral fins and it moved forwards towards the nymph. But then the fly jostling above took its fancy. The tail dipped down and the head upwards. Out of the water emerged the snout. As the jackfish jaw widened the pearly white of its gaping mouth lay exposed. My fly was engulfed. The jaws closed. The head tilted down and tail lifted.

Striking At The Right Moment

Striking fish at the right moment is one of the most difficult acts in trout fishing. To hesitate? To strike immediately? To watch for an indicator? To wait for a fish to turn? The variables are numerous. They all have one thing in common — they require visual interpretation. On this occasion I was afforded such a marvellously close and clear perspective there could be no error. The fly had disappeared, the jaws were together, the fish was horizontal. I lifted. As if stung the fish dived furiously but as the first run eased final victory seemed imminent. Success in this situation lay entirely in placing the fly on the water. In most circumstances this part of the act is only the finale of the cast, the culmination of all that's gone before.

The ultimate test of a fly fisher's skill is whether or not his fly is taken by a trout. Rejection, the bane of all anglers, can be the result of poor fly selection. But equally often (and equally the source of angling misery) the trouble is poor fly presentation. Floating line landing too close may alert a trout as might one landed somewhat less than softly even some distance away. A fly inappropriately placed is often left untouched too — it may be too distant to be attractive, too far to one side or even to the rear. The fly may float on its side or maybe upside down. Drag, variously manufactured, may render a fly unnatural or tippet nylon could kindle suspicion.

Our task in dropping the fly onto the water is to imitate a natural offering. We must attend to our gear — and we must watch the trout. How far is it moving? What is it feeding on? What obstacles surround it? What variations in current stand out in the immediate vicinity. The web of variables which must be assimilated instantly is intricate. Concerning your gear. How heavy is your nymph? Will it sink? Will your nymph drop heavily? Will your fly float high? How long is the leader? Will the floating line land lightly? Will it land close to the fish? Is there any wind? Again the possibilities are numerous — but must be attended to.

How It Should Be Done

Putting the fly down encompasses action from the beginning of the final forward rod stroke to a point where, awaiting inspection, the fly or nymph rides at the mercy of the stream. For success to be achieved it must be assumed that the last back cast rode high and straightened completely. If this is so the forward stroke should be a formality and can be achieved as follows:

During the previous upstroke, the wrist and forearm locked together and tensed in arcing the rod tip backwards. When the rod stopped (near vertical) the forearm relaxed while line and leader straightened behind. Now, the forward drive mirrors the backward action almost precisely. Initially the drive is deliberate but soon accelerates. Again wrist and forearm lock and strain but this time an increasing thumb pressure adds impetus to the line. The forward cast ends with a slight snap of the wrist finally pointing the thumb just above horizontal. The rod should stop just above horizontal too (about 10 o'clock) propelling the line to a similar position ahead. Thus the fly is not propelled directly onto the water but allowed to float the last metre or so down to settle lightly.

At the same time our non-casting hand has a part to play. As the forward drive is made allow some or all (as required) of the line held loosely between hand and reel to shoot out through the fingers. You may even follow the line towards the first stripping guide with the hand.

Following down to horizontal and below when the fly has dropped.

Some Problems

Briefly that's how it should be done but it's not always quite so simple. Commonly one error leads to difficulty in achieving a satisfactory drop. The problem begins not prior to the final forward drive but in the final back cast. It's evident in the technique of so many novice anglers. It's not exactly a conscious action but a subconscious one motivated by a desire for extra power, knowing the fly drop is to follow.

What happens is that the fly is successfully controlled in the air. The line drives back then shoots forward. The action is repeated, again with success. But then the angler decides the next cast is the one to put down. In an effort to be assured of forward power he or she dips the rod tip a little lower behind. As a result the power arc widens, the forward line speed dissipates too early and full leader (and even line) extension is impossible. The fly falls short of its target.

Lack of line speed, rod too far back leading to poor line control.

Back cast allowed to straighten. A good foundation for a successful forward cast and fly drop.

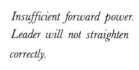

Insufficient forward power. Leader will not straighten correctly.

This error is a result of misunderstanding the link between high line speed and a small power arc, a lack of understanding of rod dynamics. It's the rod, and the tip in particular, which propels the line and fly and not the angler's arm.

I remember one friend who was learning to cast. He could exercise air control time after time. His line would shoot forward and straighten just above the water then rise quickly back in his up cast. But then, the foundations well set, he'd drop the back cast every time when ready to drop the fly. He knew he was doing it, but he couldn't break the habit. His early solution to overcome the difficulty, he told me later, was to delude himself. He'd pretend to back cast normally as if to continue in the air, then he would completely change his mind and execute a drop. A small percentage of the time it worked, but in the long term, it was not a solution. Perhaps a better decision would have been to consciously stop the rod earlier than usual. The result may be in fact that it would stop (as before in those satisfactory back casts) where it should — a mental compromise and hence a good foundation for the last drive forward.

The second problem I have observed with many anglers in executing a delicate, controlled, accurate drop is also born in the back cast — and the final back cast in particular. The difficulty involved timing. When a fast whippy rod action is employed, line control is not usually fully achieved — especially when a reasonable line length is involved. A possible reason is the fact that the line is not given time to straighten. Because it doesn't straighten, part of the power of the following stroke is removed. In addition the balance and direction of the next stroke can be affected and wind knots and tangles manufactured.

I've just mentioned the problem of the back cast lowering being accentuated immediately prior to the final drive — well, the same anxiety and exaggeration of error, exists in not allowing that reverse

Poor technique.
Not enough forward power
to extend the fly.

line to straighten. During false casts the action can usually be seen as reasonably punctuated and deliberate but, being conscious the fly is dropped, our angler holds the last back cast less than previously — or doesn't pause at all. The gap between desired result and actual result widens. The target, the fish, grows safer.

If you find that your floating line drives directly onto the water, with little or no leader extension, you can be reasonably sure you've committed the third error common to beginners. The fault results through the rod being stopped too late too low — usually somewhere below horizontal. By stopping the rod higher the leader is given time and space to straighten. Then leader and line can float down gently, undetected to the water.

During the final forward drive the non-casting hand must not be forgotten. Its duty is to release, in a controlled manner, some or all of the loosely coiled line being held. At this stage I find one large loop hanging freely to the water is easiest to control. The amount of line released will depend on the distance required in the cast and the power applied by the rod. Usually all will be released but this is not essential. What is important is that the left hand remains in contact with the line.

I watch some anglers who let the line snap free of their hand. The reason, I suspect is that there is then one less friction point affecting forward speed and with wet hands and sticky line this can be significant. The result, though, is a temporary loss of control. In addition, in reaching for the line, visual attention can be removed from its proper place — on the fish. Thirdly, in reaching for the line, an angler may lean forward. When he or she straightens up the rod may pull back, then the line, and ultimately the fly or nymph will be gently moved — usually at a most critical stage, close to the fish.

The habit of leaning forward often accompanies the final forward drive too, another subconscious effort to gain extra distance with fly. The body bends at the waist while the arms are fully straightened. That in itself is not unacceptable but an immediate straightening of the body and relaxing of the arms may be. In that case the backward movement is transferred to leader and fly.

The Length Of Line

Assuming all the mechanics of the final cast are correct it is important at this stage to accurately determine the length of line to cast. Ideally the floating line should land behind the fish, out of sight, beyond detection, while the fly or nymph should descend to a position where it can drift to the fish and be presented as desired. To achieve both of these ideals, in my opinion, suggests the need for reasonably long leaders (say a rod length and a half). In Chapter One I discussed fly placement — whether it should be left or right of a feeding trout, or over its head. In the present context some specifics of distances are now appropriate and will add to previous information.

I'm viewing the situation as a fisherman casting to a trout from

The "Bow and Arrow cast", for really tight situations.

a downstream location. This means that the river is flowing towards the angler. And remember the importance of that first cast. It would be easy to say that the best position to land a fly (or nymph) is about a metre ahead of the trout and slightly to one side. Often this is so. But flow patterns vary as does the depth at which fish feed — such differences imply changes in technique and fly placement in particular.

Perhaps I could begin with the places which it is less advisable to aim for. Certainly behind a fish is not advantageous — often this means the fly or nymph goes undetected, although that's not always so. I've watched fish turn to chase misdirected casts landing seemingly beyond sight. The dangers in causing a fish to turn are that it immediately assumes a "front-on" position and has the angler directly in sight. The fish also moves closer and, if it does take, it is, for some time, facing the tightening arm, making a positive strike more dubious.

I'd advise an angler not to land his fly directly to the side of a trout either. The fish will see such a fly no doubt but with the current moving towards the angler the fish must turn to take — hence difficulties in striking grow. To land a fly or nymph directly in front of a fish is again not the most desirable. The landing, unless a very short drift, may not give the trout time to investigate causing it to turn downstream to complete its inspection.

Bearing all of this in mind it should be becoming apparent that the ideal placement of fly or nymph is one that does not alarm the fish, allows the fish to inspect, allows the fish to take while still facing away from the angler, yet drifts the fly or nymph close to its target.

To a trout feeding in shallow water or searching close to the surface the metre ahead rule (and slightly to one side) will not be far astray. But greater latitude is necessary to a trout foraging at greater depths.

Allowing the backcast to straighten, the foundation for a good fly drop.

In this situation the nymph (usually) needs to land further ahead. Bear in mind at this time that the deeper a fish feeds the wider its upward vision and the better its chance of seeing floating line land. A longer leader, with its problems in casting, may be one answer.

Knowing that nymph (or fly) is to be placed a metre or a metre and a half ahead, is one thing — actually achieving it is another. Many anglers attempt to accomplish this through judging the line length while it is in the air during false casting. I've found this frequently inaccurate, the margin of error increasing with increasing distance between angler and fish. I employ a systematic approach, a step-by-step measuring technique.

Consider a trout 14 metres directly upstream. Starting with four metres of floating line, I flick it forward and place it down — with the delicacy I would use to a fish. Immediately I know the accurate distance between fly and fish. Then I strip a metre of line from my reel and cast once more — again putting the fly gently down. Again I can see precisely where the fish lies and where my fly is landing. After three such casts my fly should be reaching an easily estimated distance behind the trout. That extra line required for correct placement can then be removed from the reel and the first real cast made. Where space allows a trial cast may be made *well* to the fish's side to check on distance. The trial casts behind must be soft. If a weighted nymph is in use its entry to the water can be detected by a trout from a considerable distance. Those trial casts to the side too sometimes demonstrate surprisingly the fantastic eyesight possessed by trout.

Trout fishing is a complicated sport which amuses, entertains, satisfies yet continually perplexes too. Just when an angler overcomes one problem and feels real progress has been achieved his growing pedestal of pride topples sideways. Wind is such a leveller. It sends new chums homewards, would-bes to shelter and transforms garrulous experts into red-faced blunderers who rapidly seek solitude beyond the eyes of those who had observed them.

Dealing With The Wind

Wind affects all facets of our casting but it's most frustrating at the time we attempt to put our fly down. Casting on a windy day, no matter what the direction, is not easy but a few simple pointers may help a novice angler to experiment further and lead to greater success.

A tail wind is undoubtedly the kindest to a fly angler. Back casts require care, and look untidy, but ahead leaders straighten beautifully. This may allow the flexibility and safety of using a longer leader. However there are also some implications for the final cast. With the wind pushing on the leader and the line, the rod should be stopped higher than it would be in calm conditions otherwise it will land too heavily.

The converse is true when pushing into a head wind. Shorter leaders (say three metres) are advisable for reasons of control (a wind-riffled water surface diminishes the trout's ability to detect line splash or see the closer floating line) while in the final cast the rod should be stopped lower than previously discussed. In fact when fishing into a wind the whole power arc of casting should be shifted forward. This means that false casts forward should virtually clip the water while the rod tip should never climb beyond the vertical. The wind-assisted up cast may not require previous effort but the forward drop will only succeed under great concentration and rod power.

Our capital city has, quite rightly, adopted the name Windy Wellington. I don't envy fly fishers in that district. Equally I sympathise with fishing friends in Southland who battle blows not from the westerly quarter but the westerly half. They endure days that promise calm early yet develop a fury. They battle winds that change in strength but never direction — they always blow downstream. The West Coast is often kinder, the westerly fans upstream. That's fine where rivers run true but fate, one March, placed me on a spring-fed gem which meandered seemingly devoid of destination. The creek had few pools and equal numbers of fish. The two lies I fished presented opposite problems. One faced east. The other lay almost parallel.

The breeze may generally favour an angler on the Coast but the rain it bears swells and muddies rivers. It was to escape the turmoil of swollen main streams that I sought the comparative clarity of a short, groundwater-fed catchment. They're numerous on both sides of the Alps. Characteristically their beds hold fast with algae-covered stones housing aquatic fauna in abundance. Watercress, elsewhere brittle and vulnerable, carpets stream fringes while long, spindly-stemmed copper weeds, push their oval leaves to the surface, hiding considerable water depths. Waving continuously in the flow, alongside

A "Parachute cast", leader does not extend fully but falls semi-vertically to a loose snake, good to reduce drag in variable flow.

copperweed, milforts hover too while elodea, clumpy by nature, clings to gravel floors deflecting the flow and moulding a broken bed. All in all an ideal environment for trout.

Damselflies and dragonflies, with their punctuated flight, suggest juvenile forms below living alongside herbivorous snails, caddis, and mayflies. All the signals of the healthy food chain exist from simple plant and animal forms, to shags and herons graceful in flight, beauteous in form but grim in intent.

As I neared the first pool, another shower drifted in from the west. A few drops at first then a more typical Coast deluge. Distantly, against far hills, the sun still shone. Through a moistened sky, not one but two brilliant rainbows probed the earth. The inner, brighter and narrower, bore vivid deep colours, mirrored in its dominating accomplice.

My attention, waning momentarily, returned to the water. I was glad of a tail breeze at this time as the surface-rippled stream no longer sustained a glassy window atop. My choice — to wait for the rain to ease (on the Coast?) or fish blind. Fishing blind is infinitely easier with the wind behind. Already geared with a four-metre leader, dry fly indicator and small nymph I wasted little time. There's something slightly mysterious about fishing in the rain. The depth, the inhabitants, everything below remains unsighted. The sky, lower and darker, adds a mystical cloak, creating a closeness. It all adds to an inevitable meeting — the excitement lies in when.

My eyes stayed glued to the dry fly which led the nymph below. One cast. Nothing. A drift over nothing? Past a fussy one? Who knows? I probed more. Along the weeded edge, down the middle, to the other side. I moved forward, towards the eye. Attention ebbing? Luckily no. Suddenly my dry fly dipped, one moment high and visible then gone. Up came my rod, stopped abruptly, then buckled forward in submission. With the fish securely hooked I felt success was completed — a success due largely to careful casting with the wind. On each forward stroke the rod had stopped high offering the line to the breeze. Keen and true it had pushed fly and nymph down, occasionally drifting them lightly sideways, buoying them, but always cushioning them to the water.

As I traced the stream through a tight curve, circling tall flaxes securing the bank there, the breeze transformed to a wind. It always appears so to an angler like the steepness of a bridge approach to a marathon runner or the difficulty of the black ball to a pool player. I looked at the length of my leader, clung desperately to my hat then sat down to make adjustments — to shorten my leader.

By the time the nylon had been reduced to three metres, nymph and fly secured, I realised the shower had passed so between gusts some sight into the water was possible. An ancient kahikatea towering above rustling toi tois offered, in its shadow, a clearer window too. No blind casting this time. Two steps forward, stop, look. Another two steps. I avoided foot watching, streamside distractions and kept my eyes waterwards seeking to cross that bridge between looking and single-purposed, concentrated searching. The transition achieved, then success. Mid-stream, at the pool head, below a drop off, in half a metre of water a shape swayed. The stream stretched wider there, metres across.

Usually, once a fish has been sighted, the angler realises that bankside obstructions aplenty occupy his side of the stream. Limbs grow above, branches reach waterwards in front. Not so this time — clear behind, some short swampy reeds hugging the water's edge only ahead. The wind apart, no excuses. Without watching, I knew my back casts stopped vertically, straightened obediently, as they should, but there all grace and perfection ceased. Each forward thrust, despite a lower sharper stop, saw the fly line straighten onto the water followed by leader and fly which powered forward too, initially well ahead, but at the last moment, caught by the wind curled backwards to settle short.

I could have gained another metre by pushing down more heavily but instead chose another technique. Three to four metres of stream lay between the fish and the bank. By pushing more floating line forward, almost abreast of the fish but well to its side, I could use the wind to curl my fly across. A couple of paces sideways, angling slightly to the wind would help too. I waited for a brief lull. And brief it was — but long enough to flick up once. Then I drove my rod forwards stopping it horizontally. The line laid out clearly left of the fish; the fly, well ahead in the air drifted back and sideways. The nymph plopped almost on the trout's nose. The fish had to turn to take. I cared little, just rejoiced in a difficult achievement.

From the moment the last cast was initiated until the fish was struck maybe six or seven seconds elapsed, no more. But leading to those moments, considerable care in approach, tackle preparation and strategy in casting and fly placement had taken place. As mentioned before, that final fly placement, the last drop is the pivot, the link to fortune or failure.

Earlier in this chapter and throughout this book, an angler's concentrated attention on the fish is emphasised. In casting an angler must be aware of the whereabouts of rod, line and fly at all times. But with practice, and plenty of it, the casting routine can become more subconscious, automated. The final act in casting is putting the fly down. This can only be accomplished with finesse if the foundations are soundly set. With a high final back cast, a prolonged pause, allowing good line straightening the forward drive, correctly directed and stopped, should produce a good basic cast.

Now hold your breath — the real excitement begins.

5

Control On The Water

On the one and only time I've had the privilege of meeting a certain well-known hunting and fishing guide from Turangi, a lively discussion ensued about nymphing technique on the Tongariro and other streams in the Taupo area. I must admit to asking a few rather curly questions as I was meeting with little success on the big ''T'' at the time. Admittedly, the fishing generally was poor with the river running extremely low for the time of year. The rainbows stuck dourly to the bottom of the bigger pools, waiting impatiently for the next decent fresh in order to continue the spawning run.

Line gently snaked upon the water.

A few key points emerged from our convivial conversation and they have stuck very firmly in my mind. He made some comments which went something like this:

1. Good line control is vital. In his own words, ''No self-respecting rainbow will take a nymph that is moving sideways.''
2. A long, drag-free drift over the likeliest lies should be achieved wherever possible.
3. Be aware of variable current flows and mend line accordingly.
4. Upstream fishing, whether with nymph or dry fly, is a dynamic activity demanding intense concentration and an ability to adapt to changing circumstances. Again, to use his words, ''Watch the real experts at work. They are working their rod tips all the time the nymph is in the water.''

While I have some reservations about excessive line mending, especially when fishing for browns with the dry fly, I generally agree with his ideas and will refer to them later in the chapter.

Perhaps the key point is in the chapter title: ''Control'', which implies that the angler is exerting that control in a close liaison with the flow of the river, and in direct visual contact with the fly or nymph.

Let us set up a scenario. Our angler has successfully stalked a visible trout, a brown I fancy, and one which is feeding well just a little below the surface some two metres out from a bouldery bank. The fish is clearly in a feed line between two large, outcropping boulders which deflect food items nicely to the trout's position some metres below the boulders. Basically then, the fish is in a pocket, as a distinct colour difference is obvious in the stream bed at this point, the stones less visible through the mysterious, green translucency of the water. Had the fish been nymphing right on the bottom, merging with the large, even-shaped stones a metre down it would have been very difficult to detect.

Our excited angler fumbles with sausage-fingered hands and hurriedly replaces his Pheasant Tail nymph with a delicate, gossamer-winged Greenwells Glory dry. A hasty anointment with fly floatant, a shake and a blow through pursed lips to dry it, and our now very nervous angler is ready to commence battle. He considers his position in relation to the trout carefully. While apparently far enough away to avoid detection by such an avidly feeding fish, he is concerned about the dead, slack water between the shore and the feedline.

Eagerness overcomes caution. With an earnest plea to someone "up there" the potential deceiver is sent on its way. Perfect. The fly alights on the water a metre or so above the fish's position and sails jauntily down towards the waiting predator. With heart in mouth our hopeful can hardly believe his eyes when the oh-so-desirable spotted beast rises perceptibly in readiness to intercept its prey. But no. Disaster. At the last possible moment the trout pulls back from its intended course of action, hesitates momentarily and dives for cover, swallowed up amongst the multihued stones in an instant.

"But I did everything right," bemoans our unlucky angler, "A perfect cast, the fish hadn't seen me. What did I do wrong?"

Without actually being there I'd suspect that the dead water between angler and feeding line was the culprit. Perhaps our angler was so intent upon the fly's position that he forgot to strip in line and allow for the vagaries of current differential. There may have been other factors. Perhaps some undetected quirk of current in the feed line was responsible? Maybe a tiny wisp of breeze took hold of the high floating dry? Almost certainly, for whatever cause, the fly was affected by the anglers's No. 1 enemy — drag. The trout, arguably the wiliest of all freshwater fishes, simply was not convinced that the offering was a natural insect because the fly moved unnaturally. Elementary, my dear Watson, but in all honesty how many anglers

Stripping line with left hand.

really counter the effects of drag successfully all the time, I wonder?

We all lose minor skirmishes such as the one I've described. Sometimes we lose many in a single day. Still, we can narrow the odds. Hopefully, this chapter will provide a few ideas for solving some of the problems which beset us. They say there is nothing new in the world of fishing for trout. We have only to go back to the writings of old Izaak and Cotton to appreciate that. All the same it sometimes helps to take stock and attempt an analysis of some of the aspects which are normally glossed over.

In January 1988 I had a mortifying experience, one which still figures largely in my dreams, or even takes the form of a nightmare. I recount it here though as I feel that it will illustrate a vital point.

Brendan Coe, editor of *Rod and Rifle* magazine, Hugh Cooper, a Marlborough run-holder and myself were fortunate enough to find ourselves on one of North-West Nelson's prime back country streams. On the first day of blue skies and gentle breezes we saw plenty of fish and caught a few each, the most notable being one of more than three kilograms landed by Brendan.

On the second day we decided to explore downstream from our base. It was a poor decision in some ways as we found ourselves in a series of gloomy, cliff-bound pools still not touched by the sun. So we decided to head back up to the camp and from there fish upstream over the same water as on the previous day. Just below the camp we clambered up alongside a long staircase of water created by the huge boulders of an old earthquake slip which inclined steeply upwards at a neck-wrenching angle for over 1000 metres. At the very top of the watery staircase was one pool which could hold a fish, and sure enough, right on the bottom, maybe ten metres down, was a monster. We sat high above the pool and speculated on the size of "Jaws", seemingly quite convinced that it was perfectly safe from predatory anglers. Even as we watched though I fancied I saw it move upwards in the water to take something. Brendan agreed, and promptly suggested that I clamber out onto a submerged rock at the tail of the pool and have a go. I resisted the urgings for a while until the great fish rose like a submarine from the depths and began feeding from one side of the pool to the other about a metre down. I needed no more urging and somehow braved chest-deep water and a current determined to knock me off my feet to gain a precarious perch on the rock. With great difficulty I managed to stand up on it in knee-deep water.

The casting was difficult because of the high, nearby bank, covered with tangled coprosma but, with the help of a moderate upstream breeze, I was able to get my size 10 Greenwells Glory on the water just above the trout, after a couple of casts had dropped short. I was at the absolute limit of my modest casting ability, but with an inspired effort I managed to drop the fly where I wanted it. "Jaws" came right up and literally placed its nose on the fly before rejecting it and continuing to feed on the natural of its choice.

I tried again, this time with a size 12 Adams with exactly the same result. By now I was aching with the effort of staying on my rock, but with great difficulty I cast up again, this time with a large Molefly. My luck just wasn't in. As I cast a gust of wind took the fly a little sideways. I frantically tried to gain sight of it, and for a few split seconds took my eyes off the fish. Finding the fly again I looked for the trout. In the microcosm of time it took to do this, Brendan yelled, "Strike, it's got it." Out of the corner of my eye I saw the splash as the trout took the fly down. Too late. I felt the weight of the fish and then — nothing.

I made light of the incident to my companions, but inside I felt sick all day as I knew that I'd blown my chance of catching a truly big fish, and on a dry fly to boot, one of my great ambitions.

Knowing Where The Fly Is

Out of this sorry tale there comes a salutary lesson, and the first main practical point of this chapter — the need to know where the fly is in relation to the fish. My error in the aforementioned tale was failing to keep tabs on one or the other. Admittedly the situation was made more difficult by the fly being blown away by the wind to a position well away from where I expected it to be. By the time I'd picked it up visually the fish had moved out of position and the ruffled surface of the water obscured my vision. In retrospect I should have kept my eyes on the fly the whole time.

Another major error was allowing slack line to accumulate. Had I maintained tighter control I may still have effected a solid hook-up when I reacted to the splash of the take.

This business of maintaining visual control is so vital, especially when fishing the nymph when it is the fish which must be watched (or the indicator if one is being used). It is essential to make one's mind up about this. There is no point in using an indicator if the angler elects to watch the movement of the fish instead. In short, it requires a cognisant determination to watch either fly, fish or indicator.

Fishing "Blind"

I fish the Motueka River extensively, and when I fancy conditions are right, even in winter, I fish a dry fly "blind" with confidence. In a river with such a high fish population it is impossible to spot more than a tiny percentage of the available fish. Indeed, even in perfect spotting conditions, I spook plenty.

When fishing "blind" it is vital to maintain visual contact with the fly. To this end I favour a fly with at least some light colour, perhaps in the wing or hackle. A particular favourite, and a very good mayfly imitation, is the Adams which I believe is of American origin. At certain times of the year, the Kakahi Queen, an excellent pattern for New Zealand conditions, and highly visible, serves well.

An excellent combination when fishing a larger river like the middle reaches of the Motueka is a dry fly/nymph combination. I favour this method when there is no obvious surface activity. With a suitable nymph on the point, and a dry fly above one has a perfect indicator for a sub-surface take of the nymph. Sometimes the dry is taken in preference. Usually the nymph is taken, signalled by the dry fly taking a sharp dip.

There are some pitfalls in the method though. The extra disturbance factor of two flies contacting the water at virtually the same time can prove sufficient disturbance to alarm a fish. For that reason it is a method perhaps more suited to slightly discoloured water, ripply water, or poor light conditions when spotting is difficult. The two flies can also be affected by variable currents with consequent loss of the dead drift effect so important to natural presentation.

The Problem Of Drag

Drag is a major enemy of the fly fisher and with all the will in the world we can do little more than lessen its impact. Some years ago I read some American research which had been very neatly summarised by Tony Orman of *Trout With Nymph* fame.

According to Tony's article, based on these findings, drag occurs in all but the most laminar of flows, which in practice almost never occurs for more than very short distances. Drag, it is attested, is perceptible to the trout even when totally imperceptible to us as anglers. I've seen too many spooked fish in my time to doubt the wisdom of that claim, based on a properly conducted study.

At times the trout can be quite forgiving, and will actually chase and take a dragging fly if feeding avidly enough to be suffering from some form of mental block. I've read of the gentle art of skittering an adult sedge imitation across the surface of a pool in the evening to induce a take. While my limited attempts to achieve this have met

An unwanted belly of line causing the fly to drag.

with a very negative response from the trout, I don't doubt that at times it does work. Perhaps a dragging wet fly in the surface film fools caddis-feeding trout. These situations are exceptions though. In most situations trout simply don't take a dragging dry fly, or a dragging nymph, even though the degree of drag is very slight.

What causes drag? Perhaps if we can isolate the factors which cause the problem we can devise strategies to eliminate some of it.

As previously mentioned, very few streams are totally laminar in flow. The vagaries of hydrography, in the form of stream bed, steepness of terrain, obstructions etc., combine to present a complex interaction of conflicting and merging currents. Our previous book, *Stalking Trout,* outlines many of those factors of which the angler should be cognisant.

Let us take an example in the form of the eye of a pool. Our observations indicate that this is usually a prime trout lie, as it is the place where trout get "first crack" at food being swept into the pool down a normally narrow, but easily identifiable, feed line just off the main current. The main current is often too turbulent for fish to hold position in, though notable differences do occur between browns and rainbows in this regard, with the latter being prepared to tolerate more boisterous conditions.

An eye occurs on a bend, and at times is formed where the river takes an almost right-angled turn. This creates problems. For one there is nearly always an area of slack water, and secondly a back eddy which actually reverses the flow of the stream.

If a fly is cast into the feed line where the trout are most likely to be lying, a large part of the fly line lies on the slack water, or else

Angler keeping rod tip low and steady for a natural drift.
Good technique.

Line being dragged down the side of a rick by faster current.

the bulk of the line is swept back upstream. Both situations cause a degree of interference with the passage of the fly down the feed line.

One possible solution to this problem is to approach the eye of the pool warily, and to make casts from a position well downstream, where possible by positioning oneself well out into the stream so as to be as directly downstream of the best trout lie as possible. By being right in the current flow it is possible to make casts which enable the fly to travel down the "dinner lane" dead drift, i.e. unaffected by the dreaded drag.

If the current is very fast, try to maintain pace with the fly by stripping in line quickly with the free hand. Takes in these situations are often savage and swift, requiring very quick reflexes.

If you must cast across slack water to present the fly to a feeding fish, great care and a high degree of skill is required to present the fly naturally and to avoid movement. One partial solution to this problem, best effected with a long fly rod, is to hold the rod high to keep line off the slower moving water, and mend downstream.

I used to have a real problem with this position on one of my favourite stretches of the Motueka River near its confluence with the Wangapeka. I would be stymied there nine times out of ten because of this drag problem. The fish were there — I'd always be able to see some of them. But, even when they were rising freely, I'd go away frustrated after putting them down one by one. Just last season I tried the method I've outlined above. By beginning my approach from well downstream of the main lie, and by following the current up I now have much more success. Sometimes I've raised three or four fish from this one 15-20 metre stretch. As soon as the fly touches the water I maintain close contact with it by stripping in line at the speed of the current. A little mending in the form of a delicate flick of the rod tip is all that's required to eliminate much of the drag.

Another possible solution to such problems is to employ the stop cast. Instead of shooting the line to straighten the leader the cast is pushed out but not shot or the forward path is stopped earlier. The leader lands in a somewhat untidy looking bunch, but most importantly is not immediately affected by drag as it would be had the leader straightened out in the normal manner. This method has proved to be particularly useful for fish lying in front of rocks or logs where drag is extremely difficult to counteract.

Poor technique. Angler lifting rod risking moving fly directly or via drag from the weight of airborne fly line.

Ideally, one's fly should cover as much potentially fish-holding water as possible i.e. a long drift. This brings me back to the Turangi guide and the Tongariro. I spent time watching some of the "guns" on the big "T". There was little doubt in my mind, after watching some of the regulars at the Breakaway or Boulder Reach, why they were successful. Long casts combined with skilful mending brought deserved rewards.

Long Leaders

One of the secrets of achieving long drifts is the use of long, well balanced leaders. While, on the Tongariro the main purpose of five-metre leaders is to get a heavy nymph down to where the fish are presumably lying, there are other reasons too. One, of course, is to place the thick hawser of the floating line well away from the fish. But the other, perhaps less understood reason for doing so, is to lessen drag. A thin nylon leader is far less at the whim of the current than a thick, weight-forward floater, for example.

There is another very good reason why serious upstream fly fishers use long leaders. They actually force you to cast from a position well away from where the visible fish is lying, or the most likely lie if one is fishing the water blind. If we can avoid the temptation to approach too closely to the prime spot we will succeed in spooking fewer fish.

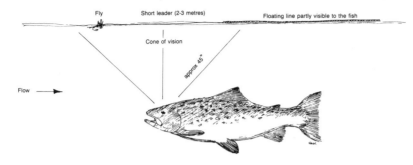

Using a short leader. Tip of floating line within trout's sight. An undesirable situation.

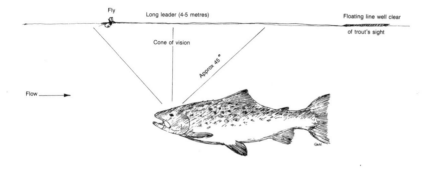

Using a long leader. Floating line outside of trout's cone of vision. A desirable situation.

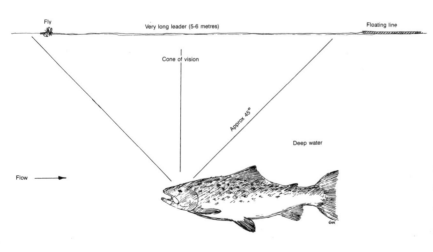

Using an extra long leader, needed when fishing to a trout lying deep.
An ideal fly leader.

Les outlines the importance of maintaining distance in an earlier chapter.

Relative newcomers with little casting experience find the handling of long leaders difficult. If it's any consolation, after many years of angling behind me, I still do, especially with shorter rods and anything above a gentle whisper of a downstream breeze. Construction of leader is very important. A suggested formula which we find successful is set out below. Except for very small waters 4-5 metre leaders are virtually mandatory.

3m — 0x or 1x Tapered leader   1m of 2kg test Tippet

Mending Line

I've used the term ''mending'' quite extensively during this chapter so perhaps we should look more closely at the practice, and the reasons for using it. Basically, mending line is the means by which we enable our fly or nymph to travel at the speed of the current, and to achieve a dead drift i.e. making the fly or nymph drift as near as possible with the natural vagaries of the stream. While this may, on paper, appear to be no big deal, it is an entirely different proposition when trying to cast a dry fly to a trout rising five metres out from the bank in a fairly fast flow of water. This situation is further complicated when there are perhaps two or more currents of varying speed between angler and fish.

I came to line mending quite intuitively, I believe, as I don't recall ever reading about the practice or being shown it by another angler. It was simply a case of ''needs must''. I believed that anyone who could handle a fly rod and line reasonably competently would do likewise. This is not necessarily so, however, as I discovered some years ago while guiding an American angler on the wild upper Buller River, where line mending is required with vitually every cast. George was an experienced angler, or so I perceived, as he talked knowledgably about techniques, rods, leaders and other angling paraphernalia on our journey to the river. We duly arrived at my chosen spot, a lovely long, boulder-studded run with relatively easy access along the bank. George was not young, and a recent hip joint replacement operation precluded any racing along the bank. It took perhaps 20 minutes or so to get tackled up and make our way to the river bed some 20-30 metres away.

Finally we made it, and I invited George to begin fishing, initially with a large weighted nymph. The idea, I explained, was to probe the pockets behind and between the boulders, all the time trying to achieve a natural drift.

''You show me how it's done,'' he urged. With no further bidding I cast obliquely upstream towards a boulder in near mid-stream. As the line came racing back towards me I stripped in line with my free hand and flipped the floater upstream by rolling the wrist, lifting the rod tip through 180 degrees in an attempt to keep the indicator drifting as naturally as possible.

"Well I'll be darned," exclaimed my client. "Now I've seen line mending for the first time."

I was quite dumbfounded by this revelation, but when I delved deeper I discovered that though the term was known, George had no idea how to apply the technique to an angling situation. The next hour was spent in some casting, or more correctly, for his casting was better than mine, line control lessons. I would dearly like to report that George went on to catch a number of fish in that run. Alas, in truth, the day was not a success in terms of fish hooked and landed, but apparently a whole new perspective was opened up to that angler on that occasion. I've often wondered how many more fish he would have landed in his long angling career if he'd applied the technique more often.

To my mind the best way to learn line mending is to spend as much time as possible on a long, evenly flowing stretch of river, fishing the small wet fly. While it is quite possible to catch plenty of fish by this method by not mending at all I believe that one's chances of success are improved by doing so. Obviously it is quite impossible to prove this contention, and I don't intend to attempt to set up an experiment to do so.

Fishing the little wet fly in the evening is to me one of the most relaxing, undemanding methods, of which I've extolled the virtues in magazine articles from time to time. The technique involves casting very slightly upstream, or at a direct right angle from the bank. Almost from the moment the fly line has made contact with the water surface a belly begins to form in the line as the faster mid-stream current sweeps it along. The trick of mending is to give a number of flicks of the rod tip, effected as aforementioned by rolling the wrist. A series of small mends will serve to flip the floating line upstream, allowing the wet fly (or nymph) dead drift until it begins to swing back across the current.

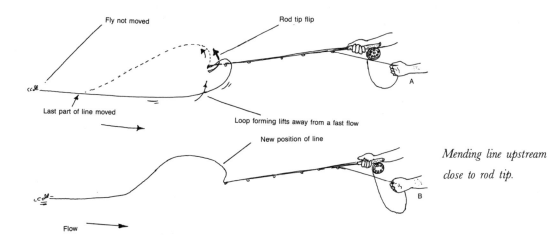

Mending line upstream close to rod tip.

Drag loop beginning to form between rod tip and water, avoid by stripping line.

Once one has a reasonable grasp of this technique it can be applied to the upstream situation, a very different and much more difficult proposition altogether, for as well as making small mending adjustments there is a need to strip in line at a rate which facilitates a natural drift. Beginners find "putting it all together" analogous to one's first attempt to drive a car. There seems so much to do all at once but not enough time in which to do it.

This is perhaps a good time to isolate these problems, and attempt solutions to them. Ultimately though, line control on the water can only be "mastered" (a term I use with great reservation) through sheer hard work, and by spending the requisite hours on the water. Written theory is at best a very poor substitute for the "hands on" approach.

I recall a chap I shall refer to as Ned who pestered me so much about taking him fishing that I finally relented one fine Sunday. Ned was a friend of a friend really, a very casual acquaintance I didn't know well at all. However, he offered the use of his vehicle so I decided that it couldn't do any harm at all to get him started. I had my doubts about him before we even hit the river. His was a forceful personality, a character who tended to impose his opinions without listening to anyone else's. He made it quite clear that mastering this fly fishing thing would probably be a piece of cake for him as he was quick on the uptake about most things. Why, he'd learned to ski in only a couple of lessons, and golf was child's play. This raised my eyebrows (and hackles) even further as I was painfully aware of the difficulties involved in the learning of both skills.

We duly arrived at a fine stretch of the Motueka and set up our gear. Ned, not short of the readies, had invested in a quality rod, reel and line as recommended by one of the local sports shop proprietors.

"O.K. then. Show us what to do," urged my eager pupil.

I stripped a few metres of line off the reel and began false casting with the enthusiasm which is always present at the beginning of the day. Gradually I extended line before plopping the small Hare and Copper nymph into the water some ten metres upstream.

"That looks easy enough," remarked Ned as he strode purposefully into the shallows and attempted to emulate my modest cast. Of course the rest of the tale hardly needs telling. Ned was simply incapable of casting even a halfway decent line. He dropped his floater in great coils, smashed barbs off hooks on the stones behind, hooked his jacket and became hopelessly entangled in loose coils of line and leader.

What made it worse was that he simply would not listen to advice. I make no claim to great expertise in the teaching of fly casting, but I could have helped had I been allowed. Ned became more and more frustrated and angry by the minute. When he started cursing loudly I wandered off and left him to it.

The journey home was long and largely silent. As far as I'm aware Ned sticks to skiing and golf.

The point I'm trying to make is that learning even basic line control requires time, patience, and possibly, above all, a good teacher. The Ned types will never make it because they lack a certain humility and expect results to come quickly. As most of us know, they rarely do in the world of fly fishing for trout.

Summing Up The Problems

The problems, as I see them once the fly or nymph makes contact with the water are:
1. Maintaining visual contact with the fish, fly or indicator.
2. Avoiding excessive drag.
3. Maintaining close contact with the fly.
4. Handling loose line.
5. Holding the rod in a suitable position to best effect a strike should the fly be taken.

The first two of these have been covered at some length already, but the third is one which presents difficulties to relative tyros. I'm aware of two schools of thought on keeping contact with a fly or nymph, especially the latter. A highly skilled angler I used to fish with a lot always maintained that more takes came his way if he stripped in line at a speed slightly faster than the speed of the current. I have my reservations about this, but I'm obliged to admit that I personally observed him catch an awful lot of fish doing just that.

When fishing the wet fly or lure downstream many anglers employ the very neat "figure eight" method of coiling line in the free hand. I've never attempted to become really adept at this, and still prefer to simply drop the line in the water at my feet — messy, but just as effective I feel. When fishing upstream into fast water there is simply no alternative, as line has to be drawn in quickly, and I mean quickly. The only serious drawback is the annoying tendency to step into a coil of line, a situation which can produce some interesting gymnastics when a fish takes and makes a wild run across the pool!

One of the most critical skills that a fly angler must learn is this knack of maintaining near contact with the fly. I believe that being just a little behind rather than in direct contact is the more effective method, for to be right with the fly one must inevitably interfere with the dead drift, so important to avoid imparting drag.

I see a surprising number of experienced anglers who fail to strip in line effectively. They find themselves in all sorts of predicaments with a belly forming in the water downstream of the angler, causing the fly to race across the current as it approaches the near bank.

As many anglers have discovered a take can occur at any point during a fly's progress, and even when well downstream of the angler. I've hooked many fish with a nymph when I've been preparing to lift line off the water to begin another cast. Once I actually hooked and landed a magnificent 2.5 kilogram hen which took a dry fly just as I began to lift the line, outstretched below me in readiness for another cast, an occurrence as fluky as downing a running deer with a head shot I fancy.

Usually keep the rod tip low and follow the fly with the tip.

It is very important to fish the cast right out, especially in broken water where visibility is difficult for both angler and fish. Many anglers make the fatal mistake of lifting the fly off the water too soon, thereby spooking the fish or not giving any others in the lie a look at the fly. Watch the fly or indicator like a hawk until it is well below your position, and keep mending that line right up until it swings across the current.

At this point some readers may be expressing doubts about the validity of some of the fairly bold statements I've been making here. "Why then," you may ask "does a fish chase and take a small wet fly swinging across the current?" A good question, and not one for which I have a truly logical answer. As stated previously it is my contention that more strikes come from a fly which is not unduly affected by drag, if at all. In my experience, based on many hours of wet fly fishing on the Motueka River, strikes occur mainly at two points in the drift process. The first, but less common, is shortly after the fly has alighted on the water, and is floating dead drift in the surface film. At this point the fly is affected by drag to a negligible degree, and if the trout are feeding well it will be taken as a nymph struggling in the surface film.

The other most common point for takes is the so-called pivot point, just as the line and fly begin the swing back across the current. While I know many anglers will disagree with me I contend that the beginning of the swing causes the fly to lift perceptibly, thereby inducing a take from a fish in the vicinity, or from one which has actually followed the fly down, possibly out of sheer curiosity. The sudden lift is sufficient to convince the fish that its prey is about to break through the surface film and make good its escape. Now this theory is not new by any stretch of the imagination, but I believe it to be a rational one. If this is so, then it can be seen that the fish did not actually take a dragging fly at all but one which was acting naturally.

On the other hand, of course, I am firmly convinced that trout take a large Taupo style lure fished on a sinking line as some kind of small fish. In this case it matters little if the "fly" is seen by the trout to dart sideways.

Stripping In The Line

But away from this digression, and back to the actual stripping in of line when a fly has been cast upstream, which is the method of fishing we are largely addressing in this book. I recommend the following procedure for righthanders:

1. Avoid the temptation to lift the rod from the position it has ended in once the line has been shot and the fly is on the water. Ideally, the rod should be about the 9 o'clock position. A very common fault with less experienced anglers is to lift the rod quickly to an acute angle. This practice produces two main impediments to

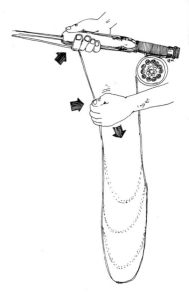

Stripping line

a successful strike and hook-up. The first is to exacerbate our old problem of drag, especially when using short leaders or if one is fishing from any sort of elevated position like a bank, log or rock. As the rod is lifted the resultant loop of line has weight, enough weight to drag a dry fly, and more importantly to alert the quarry that something is amiss. Remember, the first few seconds after the fly has landed on the water are the most vital of all. Another difficulty encountered when the rod is lifted high too soon is that there is simply not enough leverage available to set the hook should the fly be taken.

2. Strip in line with the left hand, but allow it to run across the index finger of the rod hand so that it can be clamped down on should this be necessary.

3. At all times point the rod tip at the fly without altering significantly the angle of the rod. If necessary move the body sideways, again pointing the rod tip at the fly.

Once the cast has been fished right out or the fly is well past the actual fish which has been targeted it is time to prepare for another cast. While the mechanics of this action have been explored in some depth in an earlier chapter it is perhaps pertinent to mention a point or two which may assist the beginner angler. Simply lifting dead line straight off the water, especially in a strong current can become quite a tiring task. I find it easier to pull in a few metres of line, and to employ a roll cast to lift the line from the grip of the surface tension. There really is quite a knack to this, and it is much easier to demonstrate than describe. I note with interest that no two anglers apply quite the same technique, so there is certainly no ''right'' way to achieve the one objective. Still, I believe that this is a very neglected area, and one which needs practise, just as much as the forward cast does.

Pivot point of short fly drift, when fishing from a side on position across a line of current change.

Sometimes you can get better control with the rod held high and line off the water out of faster current.

Well, where are we at? Let us return to the subject of this chapter — struggling against the odds to achieve a consistent degree of line control on the water. You should certainly not feel despondent. All of us win a few and lose a lot. This is part of the great levelling experience which is angling for trout.

As I write this I have vivid memories of a recent trip into a favourite back country gem. We fished a small tributary stream, difficult of access and rarely visited. For all I know we may have been the first anglers there that season. We certainly observed no signs of recent human activity, though any footprints would have been obliterated by the flood which had swept through only days prior to our visit.

The fish were there, not in great abundance mind, and not of massive proportions. They were hungry after the recent freshes, though, and fed avidly in every significant pool. While our party of experienced back country anglers met with lots of success, we also found ourselves stumped by more fish than I care to mention. Upon analysis, the reason, in virtually every case, related not to pattern or size of fly, for these back country beauties have catholic tastes, but to whether or not the fly (or nymph) had been affected by drag. The key to success, we feel is to be able to predict possible drag-causing factors before beginning fishing, and then to position oneself in the optimum place before making the vital first cast.

Given the vagaries of stream topography, and the self-imposed limitations of the rather primitive equipment we arm ourselves with it is not surprising that the ultimate drag-free drift is difficult to attain. Even in these high tech days of graphite rods, high floating lines and gossamer-thin nylon leaders we are not as well equipped as we may think to tackle these wonderful, ever-vigilant fish. Perhaps this is as it should be, as we have done almost too much, I feel to narrow the odds between angler and fish. But it is comforting to recall that all the fish we succeeded in fooling are back in their watery domain.

6

Striking

In this angler's humble opinion, the greatest thrill in angling for trout is that wonderful moment when the fish actually deigns to accept the artificial presented to it. On some days of difficult water and weather conditions, coupled with spooky fish, such opportunities present themselves very infrequently, if at all. All anglers can, if they are honest, report on days which produced no takes at all. Human nature being what it is we are reluctant to recall our failures, and dwell on successes only. Such no-take days are often memorable for other reasons, but after all, the primary objective of trout fishing — despite the assertions of some angler-philosophers, is to catch fish. The fact that we may subsequently release the fish is secondary. Catching fish, fooling them in other words, is important.

Waiting for the fly to drift to the fish.

While great pleasure can be obtained from the atmosphere of the river and its environs, if I'm totally honest those experiences are peripheral, subordinate to the intensity of concentration required to induce trout to take an artificial lure or fly. While I'm inclined to relax and enjoy my surroundings more once there's been a fish or two in the net, the desire to achieve the perfect stalk, cast and strike is such an all powerful urge that, like the addict hooked on heroin, I seek so assiduously my next ''fix''. I quite frequently find myself in the situation of providing guidance for others, less experienced anglers, a situation which seems to make me even more determined to help effect a capture for them, thus sharpening and honing my concentration even more.

As well as providing the ultimate ''high'' of the angling experience, i.e. the moment of the take, correct technique in striking will greatly assist in ensuring that the fish remains well hooked until it is landed. Of course we all lose fish, and usually the big ones at that. All the really big fish I've ever made contact with have managed to elude me, unless, of course, they were not quite as big as I'd imagined. Such hypothesising aside, one of the very few indisputable ''facts'' in angling for trout is that fish will from time to time be lost, sometimes right at the moment of the take, or occasionally in a last panicking dash for freedom as the fish spots the net-armed angler. Alas, most of us can even recall instances when fish have been removed from the river, but with one desultory spasm manage to flop back into their liquid medium and swim off terrified, to inform their brethren of their horrific ordeal.

Some of these escapes are really quite inexplicable. A fish may be on for some minutes when the hook simply falls out of its mouth. On other occasions, and especially when fishing with threadlining gear and metal spinners, the "premature release" comes as the fish leaps high into the air. Conversely, I'm often amazed that a fish has stayed hooked long enough to be landed when the point of the hook has penetrated only the merest surface of membrane on lips or gill cover.

Let us hark back to our imaginary angler, poor chap, learning the rudiments of the upstream approach the hard way.

Moving on past the translucent pocket where he alerted the fish through lateral movement of the fly, he comes upon a long riffly run with water of relatively even depth and principally of laminar flow. He is immediately aware of extra difficulties imposed by the jumbled surface, but he proceeds with caution and is alerted initially by a moving shadow over the mixed boulder and sand bottom. A fish of respectable proportions is weaving from side to side, covering up to a metre in its quest for nymphs. Our hopeful ties on a size 14 Pheasant Tail nymph and begins to try for the fish.

In many ways this is a much easier situation to fish in. With relatively laminar flow, no great depth of water and a broken surface, the odds are much more heavily stacked on the side of the angler this time. All goes according to plan. The nymph is spotted by the fish on the very first occasion that it goes up above it. There is no mistaking the accentuated roll in the water, and the flash of white from the inside of the trout's mouth as it devours the deadly invention of Frank Sawyer. Our angler strikes and experiences that momentary thrill of solid, unyielding weight before the bewildered fish comprehends the deception and sprints diagonally across the run. The hook pulls out and leaves our dejected hero gazing wistfully at slack floating line drifting sadly downstream.

While there is no foolproof way of ensuring a solid hook-up, a brush-up on technique, and an awareness of the requirements for successful hooking in waters of varying depths and speeds, as well as the variation between browns and rainbows, could help to narrow the odds somewhat. As will be seen too, striking when using a nymph is quite different from fishing the dry fly. Perhaps an anecdote will illustrate this point further.

In December 1988, Les Hill, my brother Terry and I found ourselves in the happy situation of fishing a more remote river. We'd had a day to remember, with Terry landing just as many fish as Les and myself despite claiming a certain lack of expertise in dry fly fishing. In fact he'd hooked and landed the first fish of a memorable six-day trip, on his very first cast — no mean feat at all. Anyway, we were trudging wearily back to camp as a vicious afternoon wind funnelling up the narrow, bluff-bound valley had made spotting and even casting, especially difficult, when Les spotted a large brown sipping flies right off the surface in a pocket on the edge of a wide, turbulent reach. Terry was duly elected to try for the fish, and with the aid of the almost storm force gale deposited the Kakahi Queen dry directly upstream of the unsuspecting trout. As the fly drifted into its window a capacious maw broke the surface and a malevolent looking hooked jaw closed on the delicacy. Waiting until the fish had turned down Terry struck, but regrettably with a vengeance that broke the 2.4 kilogram tippet like cotton. He'd hooked the fish all right, but struck as if he was into a striped marlin on 40 kilogram gear. Les and I made the appropriate soothing noises, but also explained that "striking" in this case meant merely tightening with a steady lift, quite adequate with the flex of the graphite rod to ensure penetration by the razor sharp hook. Terry went on to explain that he was using his Tongariro technique, where a true "strike" was necessary to achieve hook penetration when fishing a long cast and a leader of up to six metres.

As the week progressed he adapted well to the technique required, even when fishing a nymph to fish which had been observed feeding sub-surface, a technique quite divorced from the Tongariro style of indicator watching. Terry certainly did not have the galling experience of another break-off during the remainder of the trip. That was my lot, though, with two fish which sounded under rocky outcrops, a totally different reason altogether.

While it is asserted that rainbows take more swiftly and savagely than browns this is not always the case. If trout, either browns or rainbows, are feeding in fast water, especially in mid-stream, both species will take with equal ferocity. It stands to reason that this should be so as the available feed is moving past very quickly, necessitating a savage, slashing take. Nowhere is this more apparent than on my home water, the Motueka. I've yet to catch a rainbow in this river, though I'm assured that a very small number, strays from a small tributary, do exist. While the Motueka is largely quite docile there are some quite significant rapids and fast runs. A favourite technique when the day is dull or the water a little murky for spotting fish easily, is to fish a small, highly visible dry fly blind up these runs, often casting up at a 45-degree angle, keeping an eagle eye on my fly the whole time. I never cease to be amazed by the speed of the take, especially of fish in the one kilogram class. If one's attention were diverted from the fly for even a split second the take would be missed and the fly ejected, with the angler none the wiser. To attain hook-ups the strike must be instantaneous. The slow, deliberate lift described earlier would simply not suffice, unless, of course, the fish literally hooked itself, as some unlucky ones must do.

Let's hark back to our hero. Why did the hook pull out? Bad luck? Possibly, as sometimes the most impeccably timed strike results in a miss. I would hazard a guess though that timing or the lack of line control, alluded to in the last chapter, was most likely the reason. Lady Luck does play a part, but it is possible to achieve a remarkably high strike rate, with a combination of skill and luck.

The Speed Of The River

A critical factor is reading the speed of the river. As I've explained, mid-current or fast water feeders do not have time to waste. They must nail their food quickly and seek yet another morsel almost immediately just to keep body and soul together. Such feeding niches, whilst productive, require great energy to maintain, especially the prime positions channelling the greatest volumes of food. Such a feed line may be only centimetres wide, with the nearby, slower water a relative desert.

In streams with a high proportion of rainbows, such as many in Otago or the central North Island, summer dry fly fishing up fast runs is exciting stuff. Rainbows are generally more inclined to feed in the boisterous water that most self-respecting browns would shun in preference for more sheltered, stable niches in pockets, or in the lee of a bank extension, for example.

Again, fishing this type of water with dry fly requires reflexes as quick as for any form of nymph fishing, and to strike means just that — a swift lift of the rod until contact is felt.

This is exciting fishing, with the unexpected always on the cards. Remember, though, trout very rarely help by hooking themselves on a dry fly. The angler has to assist the hook to penetrate the trout's tough jaw or mouth interior.

On a trip to the West Coast, in January 1989, I experienced a typical example of trout with lightning reflexes. I was exploring the middle reaches of one of the Kokatahi tributaries not far from Lake Kaniere. Though the water was crystal clear, a dull, overcast sky and light drizzle did little to boost my confidence. However, I'd been told of a mixed brown/rainbow population consisting of mainly smaller fish, so I was reasonably happy about the prospects despite the conditions. Even though it was the height of the holiday season the only other sign of human activity was the red Hughes 300 which deposited a dozen red deer carcasses on the nearby grassy banks. One load was dumped unceremoniously less than 50 metres from where I was casting into a likely lie, the shooter obliging me with a cheeky grin and a thumbs-up signal.

Initially I tried to spot fish in the normally approved manner, but despite straining my eyeballs for the best part of an hour not one fish did I see. Other tactics were called for as the water certainly looked fishy enough, so I tied on a small Red Tipped Governor, dunked it in floatant and proceeded to test the water methodically by casting into every tiny pocket and pool amongst the beautifully grained schist boulders. On about the tenth cast a fish materialised from the depths of a fast-flowing run which I would have sworn didn't have a fish in it. The size 14 fly was engulfed without ceremony. Instinctively I tightened and found the fish firmly hooked. The one kilogram brown led me a merry dance down the river. I found myself leapfrogging and bounding downstream, quite unprepared for the plucky dash for freedom this relatively miniscule fish made. Some minutes later I admired a fat, silvery brown as it lay gasping in the folds of the net. A quick flick with the surgical forceps removed the battered fly and the fish was slid gently back into the river. Obviously unfazed, the silver streak positively rocketed away to be swallowed up in the tumbling Styx. They breed those West Coasters tough.

This marked the beginning of a memorable few hours. Enough fish hit the high floating dry for me to be well satisfied. All five or six fish that I landed struck in the same fashion and fought like demons possessed by heading straight for the distant Tasman Sea. It mattered little that the biggest weighed in at a tad under 1.4 kilograms. As I wandered happily back down the track the helicopter crew was busy dumping the deer carcasses onto the tray of a truck. The shooter pointed at the two fine fish I was carrying back for my hosts at Kokatahi and repeated the thumbs up with even more enthusiasm, obviously somewhat surprised by my success.

In retrospect it became clear to me that in these conditions, with the fish feeding in the faster runs the strike had to be instantaneous. I missed a couple by simply reacting too slowly, or by not maintaining close contact with the fly. I may have missed others by not observing the take in the jumbled water. The fishing had been fast and furious demanding absolute devotion to the cause.

While I enjoyed the spectacular scenery on my way back down the valley, I was so single-minded on my journey upstream that I probably wouldn't have seen a 12-point stag if it had stepped out of the olive-hued bush.

Rainbows And Browns

Striking from a seated position, good control with left hand.

Perhaps somewhat surprisingly, all the fish I encountered that day were browns — surprising because they behaved exactly as rainbows are supposed to do, which leads me to speculate that while differences

in feeding habits and the actual taking of the fly do undoubtedly exist, the inherent nature of the stream plays a major part.

It is probably true to assert that rainbows are a little more catholic in their tastes, less inclined to be "put down" by a slight amount of drag or a sloppy presentation than browns. One has only to experience the Tongariro when the fishing is "on" to realise that rainbows are fooled by some pretty inept presentations at times. I'm assured by a former Taupo fisheries officer that there are far more browns in the Tongariro than most people realise, but it is no accident that a very small percentage of these are taken by anglers. Browns simply will not tolerate the continual procession of anglers through the favoured runs and pools of that wonderful river. Those that do succumb are invariably taken at night when the crowds of anglers are gone.

Wherever rainbows and browns co-exist it is as well to be on the lookout for the somewhat more sedentary, large browns residing in situations more conducive to easy living. Those areas, close to but just out of the full force of the current, where the food is literally served up smorgasbord style, are prime brown trout lies, even if the predominant population is of more showy, flamboyant rainbows and juvenile browns.

These fish are normally a totally different challenge, unlikely to be duped by just any old size or pattern of fly. A close imitation based on the resident stream insects is often necessary. Such fish tend to become fixated on a certain natural whether taking mainly sub-surface or right off the top.

Striking too hard.

Feeding Behaviour

Let's examine feeding and striking behavour in more detail. As explained, smaller browns may feed and behave similarly to rainbows, often taking swiftly and savagely. Larger browns, unless resident in very fast water, tend to take in a calculated, measured manner. Few sporting experiences can rival the excitement generated by a large brown as it takes in an artificial fly.

Most authorities on trout behaviour believe that trout suck in their food with a quantity of water before expelling that water out through the gills. If this is so then it is logical to believe that it would be difficult for a hook to take hold inside the trout's mouth when the fly is mixed with a considerable quantity of rapidly flowing H_2O. This is possibly why the traditional sipping dry fly rise and take requires the angler to exercise patience before tightening.

I recall vividly my early, frustrating attempts to hook trout on the dry fly. Besides having the problems of effective line control and presentation to contend with, I had great difficulty with timing once the fly had been accepted.

A good "Solid" strike.

The Strike

While nobody can lay claim to infallibility with striking, it is possible, as explained earlier, to reduce the number of total misses greatly.

As a general rule — and here I stand, likely to be hoist by my own petard — I will contend that more fish are lost at the moment of the take by striking too hastily, rather than the converse.

Of course it is easy to miss a hook-up by being too slow as well. A trout has a remarkable ability to reject and eject a fly too, though I firmly believe that there is a reasonable margin of allowable time

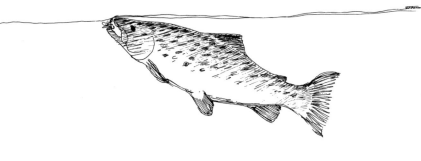

A trout rising and taking a fly — too early to strike.

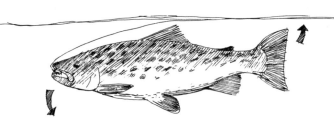

A trout beginning to turn down — too early to strike.

Time to strike — trout has turned down with fly.

Striking a fish. Lifting rod tip firmly with right arm. Pulling down with left hand.

to actually set the hook, possibly more than is often realised.

The old maxim of "One-Two-Three-Strike" is usually not too far short of the mark with dry fly in a slowly moving current. Les Hill and associates have been known to utter (quite audibly, and with no disrespect intended) "God-Save-The-Queen." Les misses fewer than most, so apparently it works.

Experience dictates though, that the delay varies greatly from the almost instantaneous, exaggerated strike in boisterous water to the measured, calculated turn of the wrist, and firm but gentle lift of the rod e.g. when fish are taking mayfly duns directly off the surface in the evening. In such situations the fish takes in a relaxed, leisurely manner. The angler should follow suit and strike accordingly.

Good technique. A firm strike with good use of left hand.

Back Country Browns

But let us return to the back country. Again, at great risk of being laughed off the stage, I'm going to take another pot shot at a sacred cow. It is my firm belief, based on many long days on back country streams and rivers in various parts of the South Island, that back country browns are easy to catch. Before I put the proverbial foot right in it let me qualify that statement and admit that some back country browns are probably the hardest to catch. I know a place in a certain river, a name which induces a temporary memory loss, where there dwells one trout which I estimate conservatively to weigh in the vicinity of six kilograms, a veritable monster considering the size of the stream. Also in the pool, or run, because I'm not quite sure how to describe it, are at least two other fish in excess of four kilograms. No I haven't weighed them, but I've looked longingly for hours, and I'm quite convinced that my estimates are not too far out.

These fish have everything going for them. Their home, about as impregnable as Fort Knox, is a long, quite narrow pool on a prominent bend in the river. As the river turns almost at right angles, deflected by a rock outcrop reminiscent of a dreadnought the whole volume is channelled via a narrow rapid into a swiftly moving pool of great depth. Through occasional ''windows'' in the surface turbulence, it is possible, when the river is low and clear, to view the larger of the aforementioned monsters. This great fish lies almost motionless right on the bottom in at least ten metres of water. In an hour of watching from a position almost directly above I never saw it move more than a few centimetres from its position. In descending order of size the underlings lay in line astern of "Big Boy", both considerably more active than their superior but still virtually uncatchable by traditional, legal means.

I frequently lie awake at night scheming the demise of this great beast, but apart from camping on location and waiting for it to take from the surface I am totally at a loss, as the surface current and lack of casting positions both up and downstream tend to make the use of conventional methods impossible. Still, I'm working on it, and in the not too distant future I propose to try a quite unorthodox, but perfectly legal method. You'll probably hear about it if I manage to fool that fish.

Conversely, given conditions of a clearing river, a bright day to facilitate spotting, and relatively shallow pocket water, I contend again that even large browns, perhaps of two or three kilograms, are easy prey compared to their smaller low country stream cousins. Back country trout are great opportunists, and much less selective (normally) than the browns of say the Mataura or Manawatu which have to be constantly on guard against predatory humans. The beauty of it for me is that these superb, wild fish can be fooled by small, traditional dry flies at virtually any time of the day. After reading much angling literature you could be excused for believing that dry fly fishing is to be attempted only at dusk, and that the only times of the day for all forms of trout fishing are dawn and dusk. Well, I'm rarely anywhere but in The Land of Nod at dawn in mid-summer, but I can assure you that dry fly fishing time in the wilds of Otago or the Central North Island is anytime, apart from perhaps the middle of the night, and I'm not even sure about that as I'm not particularly fond of stumbling and bumbling around on a river bank at 1 a.m.

Another myth which I would like to take the opportunity to debunk

A lively reaction to the strike.

is that if a trout is feeding below the surface that it will not take a dry fly from the surface. Again, bunkum. We've all read the statistics which tell us that 90 per cent of a trout's food consists of sub-surface fauna, i.e. nymphal forms, in the main. I do not for one moment dispute that, but do know that a back country brown is just as likely to take a well-presented size 14 Greenwells Glory dry as a weighted Stonefly or Pheasant Tail nymph. The low country branch of the family will quite often do so too, even if there is not a winged natural in sight. If you fancy dry fly as a more aesthetically pleasing method, then go on, make a pig of yourself, but at least be flexible enough in attitude to change to a nymph if the dry produces no reaction.

Just what do you do when that Mohaka monster lifts its great, ugly head right out of the water and gobbles your best Dad's Favourite? Well, a prayer or two imploring a certain bearded gentleman to help would not go amiss. Failing divine intervention, the best course of action is to stay calm.

"Stay calm, the man says. How can I stay calm when the trout of a lifetime has actually selected my fly from all those real ones!"

If you can't stay calm, and in all honesty, who could, then wait at least two long seconds, and without attempting to fling the fish over your shoulder, lift with a steady, continuous motion upwards and outwards at about a 70-degree angle. If you are lucky you'll soon know about it. No self respecting trout, be it brown or rainbow, likes to go anywhere unless it be of its own volition, and if it's a rainbow chances are ten to one on that it will leap clear of the river before attempting to emulate a torpedo.

In this book I do not intend to delve into the specialised and complex world of rise forms. Clark and Goddard, as well as Vince Marinaro and others have more than adequately covered this fascinating aspect of fishing for trout. With experience it is not too difficult to tell if a trout is feeding on the surface, well beneath it or just under the surface, or perhaps in the surface film itself.

Fly Or Nymph?

Again, I would like to fire a broadside at what I consider to be a myth. In this day of enlightenment very few anglers indeed persevere with the dry-fly-only attitude which was very prevalent in Britain, and to a point here too, until people like Tony Orman in *Trout With Nymph,* (to my mind one of this country's angling classics) finally convinced the diehards that they'd been missing out on a great angling experience. Still, there exist many who have widened their angling repertoire to include nymph and wet fly yet persist in believing, and perpetuate the myth, that dry fly angling is extraordinarily difficult. It simply is not, and satisfying though it may be, it does not hold a candle to nymph fishing in its pure, unadulterated form. Here I am deliberately excluding what nympher extraordinaire Jim Ring and his wife refer to as "blymphing", or "bloody fool nymphing" a la Tongariro. Enough. I'll have upset thousands by such a proclamation, and to be fair I acknowledge and applaud the skills, albeit different, of the more accomplished Tongariro anglers.

The art of stalking trout, as elucidated by Englishman, Frank Sawyer in *Nymphs and the Trout,* Tony Orman in *Trout with Nymph,* as well as in our earlier book *Stalking Trout,* is probably the most skilful and arguably most satisfying method of catching trout yet devised. We are here dealing with striking so let's examine the subtleties of hooking a trout with a nymph. Dry fly exponents are forced to completely rethink their technique when fishing by this method. Initially, the adjustment relates to the business of looking into, rather than at, the water. In some ways I must count myself fortunate as I encountered the nymphing technique at a very crucial time in my evolution as an angler with the discovery of Tony Orman's book so I had not too many pre-conceived notions, false or otherwise, about dry fly as opposed to nymph. Others were not so lucky. A very fine angler of my acquaintance, who makes no bones whatsoever about his preference for dry flies to this day, was for many years firmly convinced that to attempt to look into the water was pointless. During his angling apprenticeship he fished when the fish were rising — end of story. If there was no insect activity, and trout clearly taking food from the water surface he did not fish. Fortunately the Southland trout were usually obliging, and it appears that he caught more than his fair share by use of the dry fly alone. It was years later, fishing with Les Hill, that a whole new world of angling opened up. He now fishes the nymph with confidence and skill when conditions and feeding habits dictate.

On a day when spotting is relatively easy and trout are clearly feeding sub-surface in shallow runs, riffles and pockets, nymph fishing can be a deadly method. I've experienced many such days when the fishing has been ridiculously easy — almost invariably clear, bright

Be prepared for "Fireworks" immediately after the strike.

summer days with the sun high in the sky and the fish avidly seeking food. On such days the fish are so preoccupied that they seem less cautious than normal. Such days provide the angler with a unique opportunity to observe closely the actual take of the nymph. I contend, that providing one is observant the take is easily detected. In my opinion the following actions signal that the artificial nymph, as opposed to a natural, has been taken.

1. A flash of white as the mouth opens to engulf the nymph.
2. A distinct twisting and lifting motion — a motion noticeably different from the taking of a natural.
3. A dash to the side — perceptibly different to natural interception.

The sceptical would claim that the very same movements indicate the taking of the natural. In my opinion this is not normally so, with the possible exception of the third point above. I've often been fooled by a fish racing out to the boundaries of the feed line or beyond to snatch a natural nymph before drifting back into position. The most observant of anglers rarely spots the white inside of the mouth whilst a fish is actually taking natural nymphs sub-surface, but frequently does so when the mouth is opened to devour an artificial. Why this should be is a complete mystery to me, and not one I will even attempt to explain. The second habit mentioned is the surest giveaway of all. Even when the artificial nymph is heavily weighted with copper or lead wire the characteristic rise and roll in the water is frequently observed.

With experience, striking becomes an instinctive, reflex action with the nymph. When fishing at close quarters to a feeding fish the ''strike'', really little more than a sideways and upwards flick of the wrist, should be sufficient to set the hook. It is altogether a sharper, snappier movement than that required with the dry fly, except as explained when fishing the surface fly blind in fast, joggly water. While it is still possible to set the hook too quickly, especially in slower streams and lakes, as a general rule fish will be lost through being too slow on the strike — the direct opposite of the dry fly strike.

Accomplished nymph anglers do develop a certain instinct enabling them to hook up with quite amazing frequency, even when the fish is barely visible or not visible at all. Frank Sawyer in *Nymphs and the Trout* explains it thus.

''One develops an awareness which is not even a sixth sense. It is something which cannot be explained. You see nothing, feel nothing, yet something prompts you to lift your rod tip, some little whisper in your brain to tell you a fish is at the other end of your line. But this feeling only comes when you are intent upon your work, for though it may not be possible to see through the surface, it is possible to visualise the position of the fish, and to anticipate his actions.''

The specialist nymph angler is a joy to watch. Not for him the gaudy fluorescent lines and great plastic blobs of strike indicators. This usually solitary, highly observant angler with an uncanny ability to read the water relies entirely on his instincts and senses.

Fishing blind with a nymph is considered by many to be a fruitless, unrewarding pursuit, and so it can be too, but I recall days of astonishing success when overhead conditions precluded spotting completely. I know a shallow, bouldery stretch of the Motueka which nearly always rewards me if the river is just clearing after a fresh. I fish it blind, rarely casting more than a metre out from the bank, and using a single nymph on a 2.8-metre leader. I'll frequently fish this position when the water is so murky that most anglers would not even put up their fly rods. I probe small pockets behind boulders and watch the end of the floating line like a hawk. Should it hesitate even slightly I strike swiftly with the aforementioned flick of the wrist. I use a 2.4-metre fast action graphite rod for this work in conjunction with a weight 5 or 6 weight forward floating line.

Strangely, even though the fish are rarely visible, it is unusual to lose a fish here by mistiming the strike, so it appears that the swift reaction when the first indication of a strike is registered is the answer. Obviously, I remain blissfully unaware of those fish which take and eject the nymph. To deny that this happens from time to time is to

Striking with rod high.

admit to an indecent degree of conceit. If there is one sport where a fair dollop of humility and a good sense of humour are imperative it is angling for trout, where one is quite frequently "taken to the cleaners".

Interestingly, just when we think we have mastered this striking thing, we are often brought very firmly back down to earth by the days when nothing goes right. We probably all experience them, usually I find, when you are attempting to impress someone. I suspect that most anglers, being of a somewhat solitary inclination, are affected to a degree by stage fright when being observed, especially when the observer is expecting the "expert" (how I detest that term) to wave a magic wand and pull trout from the river like rabbits out of hats. Perhaps we try just a little too hard in such situations. Audience or not, we all experience such days when the timing has simply deserted us.

I recalled such a day in a *Rod and Rifle* article some years ago, whilst in the company of some so-called friends who obtained immense pleasure from watching me either put fish down with poor casts or miss them on the strike. As confidence waned, anxiety resulting in bad coordination due to excessive striving, resulted. At lunchtime I was despondent, morose and generally unhappy until someone produced a hip flask containing a small quantity of a fiery liquid well known to sportsmen in the more southern regions of our country, in particular. Somehow, after half an hour's rest, a few slices of salami on cracker biscuits and a thorough warming-up, both externally and internally, the world seemed a brighter place again. Within minutes of recommencing fishing I had spotted, cast to, hooked and landed a fine brown trout. I'm firmly convinced that my success this time was due entirely to a change of attitude, induced by the brief respite from the intense concentration of the stalk.

In Chapter 9 Les Hill discusses the whole subject of concentration, and with it the concept of positive mental attitude. Superb angler, guide and writer Gary Kemsley often refers to "P.M.A.", the business of going fishing, knowing that all things being equal there is a very good chance of catching fish.

Les Hill is undoubtedly the greatest adherent of this concept I've ever met, and as such is a wonderful inspiration to others. Les is never pessimistic about his chances and, come hell or high water, fishes in the certain knowledge that the fish are there, and that all we as anglers have to do is work out where, and use appropriate techniques to catch them.

This attitude can possibly be applied with greatest relevance to striking. Successful striking requires positive action, and, above all, concentration. So when the going gets tough following a series of missed takes, think positively and don't wallow in self-recrimination. Remember, it's meant to be fun. More about that later.

7

Playing Trout

Currently I find myself in a situation which must be the envy of many keen anglers. I live a mere minute's drive from the lovely Motueka River. While I can't actually see it from where I write this I can catch a glimpse of riverside willows in early summer hue. Beyond, verdant green river terraces backed by ordered rows of pines, then dense beech forest rising to the volcano-shaped Mt Crusader and bleak Hoary Head complete the scene. If I so choose I can grab rod, vest and net and be fishing a long, productive run within 15 minutes of stepping out the door.

If I desire something a little more challenging I can explore a number of wilder tributaries issuing from the Mt Arthur Range, or try to tempt the wily but prolific browns of the spring-fed Riwaka some 20 or so minutes away.

Rod kept high.

Paradise, I'm sure you will agree. Fortunate indeed is the angler who can live and work in the district of one's choice as I do. I feel a deep sense of humility in my good fortune, and genuinely sympathise with those whose angling opportunities are limited by the location of their employment. For me, the outdoor life, and angling in particular, is part of my entire reason for being. To be forced away from it for an extended period would cause me untold misery.

Many, though, are far more forebearing and phlegmatic than I, much more accepting of their situation, and while sharing my passion for my favourite sport, they temper their enthusiasm by planning and scheming fishing expeditions. Many Aucklanders put in more hours on river or lake than I do by fishing the Rotorua or Taupo region at every opportunity. They beat a path south every Friday night and return late on Sunday, tired, but happy to recommence battle with the workaday world. Others get precious few opportunities, perhaps only one or two major trips per year, but the expectation and excitement which precedes such a trip compensate handsomely for time spent away from the river.

Such an angler is Eden Shields of Auckland, a long-established member of "Hills Tours", an annual event, exploring a back country area anywhere from Nelson to Fiordland. While the other members of the party have normally had many days fishing prior to these December or January expeditions, Eden always arrives tired and somewhat jaded after another tough year of trying to make a living, a process which sometimes takes him to various parts of the world on short, intensive business trips. By December, he's really looking forward to the peace and tranquility of a mountain valley.

The term "re-charging" is somewhat clichéd, and I use it at my peril, but "re-charge" is undoubtedly the most apt description of the transformation which takes place over the ensuing days of humping heavy packs up and down rugged valleys, camping in idyllic riverside settings and, of course, catching trout.

This chapter is about the "playing" of trout, a term I'm a little uncomfortable with, but one I'll stick with because it is understood. I haven't lost sight of the chapter title despite my digressions.

One would be forgiven for assuming that our city-based friend, who I assure you is passionate about his fishing, would be spending every waking hour of his holiday attempting to fool large trout. Curiously, this is not the case. Eden actually has to have his arm twisted to fish once a fish has been spotted. Such is the pleasure and enjoyment derived from simply being there that the actual fishing becomes almost incidental.

Despite the lengthy periods when he doesn't fish, Eden's prowess with a fly rod is such that he misses very few opportunities, especially when the fish are rising to the dry fly. His timing is impeccable, born of a lengthy apprenticeship in the deep south of the South Island. Suffice it to state that very few fish are missed on the strike. At this point though, once the fish has been hooked, a very curious thing happens. He immediately tries to release the fish, or at least to land it with almost indecent haste.

"Catch And Release"

Over long, convivial campfire sessions we have discussed this penchant for "catch and release" without actually landing the fish. Eden asserts very strongly that the highlight of angling for trout is the moment of deception i.e. when the fish takes the artificial and is hooked. Unless the fish is in trophy class (he has one over 4.5 kilograms to his credit) or is urgently needed for food, Eden prefers to lose it shortly after the hook-up or land it with utmost haste so that it can be released as unscathed as possible by its unpleasant experience.

To best effect this "quick release", a number of strategies are employed, including allowing the line to go slack (usually unsuccessful even with barbless hooks), holding it on a very tight line, and the use of heavy tippets so that the fish can be landed and released quickly. If possible he avoids any actual handling of the fish. One angler I know swears by the effectiveness of employing a roll cast type of action in conjunction with barbless hooks.

As part of one's angling evolution there comes a point, for most people at least, where landing every fish hooked assumes less and less importance. I can recall being upset literally to tears at the loss of a fish, especially if it was big and the fight prolonged. This is a most natural inclination, for we surely fish mainly to catch fish. I certainly do anyway. For one thing I like to see what it is that I've been attached to.

I've been enjoying some excellent evening fishing this season, and have regularly landed two or three fish up to 1.8 kilograms, fish rising

Exerting side strain.

to mayfly duns in the last hour of daylight. One evening things had been pretty quiet until rather late when a few desultory rises began. The mayfly hatch, as unpredictable as ever this season, was soon over, and while I'd pricked one fish none had come to the net. At 10 p.m. I was about to head for home when I noticed a tiny, sipping rise right on the edge at the tail of a deep pocket, heavily overhung with willows. At almost the same instant a brown grass grub beetle blundered into my face so I immediately swapped my size 16 Adams for a Green Beetle imitation. On my second cast the very tip of a nose broke the surface close to where I guessed my beetle to be, so I tightened slowly and was heartened to feel the weight of a fish. A few minutes later a spirited little fish of a little over one kilogram and about 40 centimetres long came to the net and was promptly released.

Almost immediately I observed another tiny, sipping rise a metre or so further up. Again, the green beetle went out. By this time the rapidly descending gloom precluded any possibility of seeing the fly, and in truth I heard rather than saw the rise. Tightening more in hope than with any great expertise I was surprised to feel a series of short, solid tugs. For a split second the line went dead and then knifed through the water as an obviously sizable and rather angry trout literally shot up through the pocket into and through the rapid at the top and simply kept going. All I know is that, judging by the weight of the fish as I felt it briefly before the breakneck upstream dash, this was no juvenile. I didn't have a chance. The 2.4 kilogram tippet snapped like tying thread. I was left gasping and just a little shaky, but I didn't get upset, and with a shrug of the shoulders I wound up and stumbled back to the car, musing on just what I should have done.

With all the will in the world we lose fish, often when capture is very important to us. As I've tried to explain, the actual landing of fish tends to become less important as the years roll by, but it is nice to complete the exercise anyway, as somehow, to me it is the culmination of the stalk, the cast and the hook-up — a natural and logical conclusion.

We must assume that readers of a book such as this want to improve their catch rate, and that implies landing any trout we may be fortunate enough to hook. Let us examine some more strategies which may help us achieve this objective. After all, the Eden Shields of the world are probably very much in the minority.

If we were totally objective about this we would attempt to analyse in detail, and in a scientifically clinical way, a vastly complex myriad of possible scenarios. Not only would this prove to be painfully boring, it would also serve to confuse the relative newcomers to the sport, who may be reading this book. Anyway, it is time our unlucky hero actually caught a trout.

For once it all comes together. As the powerful graphite rod lifts to the near vertical the floating line whips off the water with a hiss. The angler is aware of a sense of being connected momentarily to something heavy but slightly yielding as well. This feeling is replaced

almost instantly by the sensation of floating line racing through hands
at a breathtaking rate. A bow wave is formed as the trout traces an
unerringly straight path diagonally upstream and across the wide,
riffly run. The reel screams its unmistakable music as line continues
to peel off at an alarming rate. Wisely the angler does not attempt
to impede this first panicking dash, but allows the line to run smoothly
between forefinger and rod. Concern is felt though when the silky
smoothness of floating line is replaced by thin, braided nylon backing
and the run continues right to the far bank.

Our hero decides that this is the time for some positive action. With
all the floating line, plus a third of the backing off the reel, something
needs to be done. With tip held high he pumps the fish and is
heartened to regain a few metres of backing. He notices that this has
the effect of forcing the fish to seek escape by moving downstream
parallel to the far bank. The angler responds by applying sidestrain
and walking downstream as well. Slowly but surely the fish is worked
back towards the near bank. In mid-stream it begins another run
and leaps clear of the water in a shower of spray, almost inducing
heart failure in our now very shaky angler who is beginning to feel
an ache in his right wrist from the constant, unrelenting pressure
he is applying to the fish with the sidestrain. Another, rather tired
leap signals the beginning of the end for the fish. It fights close to
the surface now, unable to make more than short sporadic runs. The
angler senses victory and leads the fish towards a tiny, shallow pocket
amongst the river stones. As the fish sees the angler for the first time
though it makes another vain dash for freedom, but is soon brought
under control again, led into the small bay and lies gasping on its
side in a few centimetres of water whereupon it is leapt upon and
carried higher up the gently sloping bank to be despatched by a sharp
rap on the head with a convenient stone.

The angler, exultant over his success at last, is also affected by an
element of remorse as well, perhaps an inevitable consequence of
pitting wits against such a worthy and noble beast. As he gazes at
his prize he marvels at the beautifully efficient and remarkably
camouflaged body. Success is sweet though, and if no more fish come
to the bank this day it matters not. A fly fisherman is born. Life will
never be quite the same again.

This angler did everything right. Rather than attempt to halt the
first run he kept his cool and allowed the fish to have its head. Many
anglers have learned to their dismay that it is extremely difficult to
turn a fish on that first, supercharged run. At this stage in the
proceedings the ability to control the flow of line is much more
important. If there is any chink in your armour in the form of a loop
of loose line on the reel, or if the reel is excessively tight and in need
of lubrication, then a strong fish will exploit that chink. If there is
loose line held in the hands or on the water when the fish is hooked
I find it wise to transfer line to the reel as soon as possible. Not all
anglers will agree with me on this one, and I've noticed a trend
amongst American anglers to play fish the whole time with some

metres of loose line in the water. I much prefer to have the line on the reel, as that means one less aspect to worry about.

The First Run

Giving a trout its head on the first run makes good sense even if the fish is heading for a snag. It may be possible to turn it but in the long run it is possibly better to let it go and take the chance of being able to extricate it once the initial sting is out of it a little.

I sometimes don't take my own advice here. On a recent back country trip with Les Hill I hooked a large trout (probably in the region of three kilograms) on a dry fly. The odds against landing it were stacked solidly against me from the outset as we were fishing a particularly turbulent stretch full of dining-table-size boulders. After a tricky cast over the top of one of these giant rocks I hooked the fish on the first drift over it.

"Let it go," shouted Les over the roar of the river. I chose not to take his advice as I could see that the fish was hell bent on heading for a bolt hole under one of the rocks. Instead I tried to hold it on a short, tight line. Strong leader or not, the great power of the river and the determination of the fish combined to snap the leader. I may not have landed the fish had I allowed it to run but I would at least have had some chance. Obviously, each case has to be judged on its merits, but to attempt to "horse" a fish shortly after hook-up is most unwise.

The sheer power of sometimes quite small trout on that first run never ceases to amaze me. I'm more often than not taken right into the backing on the Motueka and other broad rivers, and it is not unusual for the hook to pull out at this point. Once this initial run has been survived though, provided the hook has a firm hold a lot

A stronger tippet allows more side strain and faster landing.

of the fight seems to be taken out of the fish. It is important at this point to raise the rod high in the air, partly to allow the tip section to work with its flexibility but equally to extract any belly of line being tugged by the river adding strain on the tippet. Shorten the line as soon as possible.

I've mentioned sidestrain, and this is an effective method of tiring a fish quickly, especially if there is room on the bank to move freely downstream. Sidestrain involves inclining the rod at about a 45-degree angle and walking slowly downstream so that the fish is constantly off balance. It is important to apply firm pressure, and to counter any minor runs not so much by allowing the fish to take line, but by giving a little with the rod while maintaining about the same length of line. At times it is necessary to give line, but a common fault I observe amongst less experienced anglers is giving the fish too much freedom once the initial, very strong runs are over. This simply prolongs the whole business of landing the fish and allows more opportunity for the hook to pull out.

I believe in playing fish hard, and preferably on a relatively short line. Sometimes though, because each fish is an individual, and therefore quite unpredictable in its behaviour, it is not easy to dictate terms as one would wish. A few nights ago I was fishing the Motueka with a small wet fly right on dark. The strong sea breeze had not dropped as I'd hoped and consequently there was only a very sporadic hatch in the cold, blustery conditions. However, I'd noticed one fish rising occasionally in a small pocket below the tail of a long run, so I kept drifting the size 12 Twilight Beauty over its lie. I didn't see the take but after about ten casts I was fast into a very powerful fish which had me into the backing in seconds. The fish tore down into a fast rip lined with willows while I stumbled over the slippery, algae-covered stones in an attempt to follow.

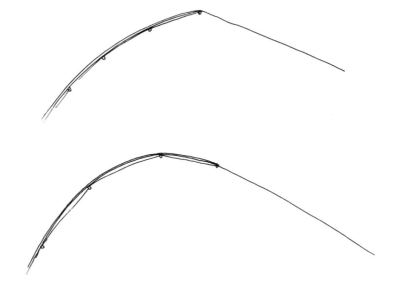

Not enough pressure on fish.

Keep a good bend in rod and plenty of pressure on fish.

Exerting side strain to lead a fish bankwards.

The willows prevented access down my bank, and the fish showed no sign of succumbing to the almost indecent degree of sidestrain I was applying, so I was forced to cross the river at this point. Had it been light enough to see, any onlookers would have enjoyed the spectacle of me almost running across the shallow rapid in an attempt to keep up with this trout hellbent on taking me down into the next major pool. The sidestrain finally took its toll and, as the fish thrashed around in the shallows, I looked eagerly for a glimpse, convinced that I had hooked into a really big Motueka brownie at last. Disappointment rapidly followed elation when I scooped up a very fat but far from record-breaking hen which would have tipped the scales at a full 900 grams. The reason for my merry dance soon became apparent though. The fish was very firmly hooked at the base of the pectoral fin. When a trout, or any fish, cannot be led around by the mouth it poses all sorts of difficulties for the angler. Perhaps the worst place to foul hook a fish is in the tail. Then you really have a battle on your hands.

Not just foul-hooked fish fight unpredictably. Despite fairly frequent assertions to the contrary, even brown trout will sometimes spend as much time battling for their freedom out of the water as in it. We find that particularly well-conditioned back country trout are great leapers. This calls for a rather special playing technique, one which is learned from experience rather than from books, and involves following the fish with the rod tip with each leap. It is possible to be able to predict with some accuracy just when a trout is about to leap. Often the signal for this is a dash downstream followed by a few short sharp jolts just immediately prior to the jump. Break-offs frequently occur due to unpreparedness for the jump, especially if the fish succeeds in landing on the leader. Nearly all trout hooked with spinning gear jump at some stage, and in the majority of cases throw the hook during one of these gymnastic performances. There is little disputing that trout hooked on a small fly hook are much more likely to stay attached, than those hooked on a treble attached to a Toby lure, for example.

Allowing a fish to run.

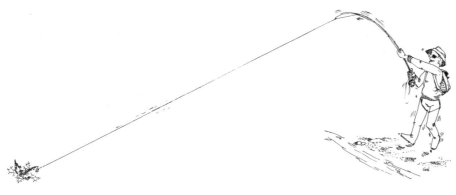

Exerting sidestrain and walking backwards to lead a fish to the bank.

A disconcerting habit of a minority of trout, once hooked, is to actually swim towards the angler. This is much more likely to happen in still rather than moving water, but it does occur in rivers too from time to time. All the angler can do in this situation is to back-pedal quickly and strip in line with the free hand. I've quite frequently encountered this situation, but invariably have managed to recover the position sufficiently to avoid losing the fish. One consolation is that the fish will soon place pressure on the line once it sees the angler and, as long as it does not run between the angler's legs, can be played in the normal fashion.

I once had an hilarious experience on the Tongariro. I was fishing the bottom end of the Blue Pool, and was fortunate to connect with a fish, only my second for the day. In typical Tongariro fashion the fish scorched off for the far side of the pool and straight between the legs of another angler (clad in full body waders) fishing up the far side. I don't think the other chap was particularly amused, especially as he'd been flogging the pool for some time without success, and I'd only just arrived. Luckily, he was able to extricate himself from my line fairly easily, and I went on to land the fish, a very fat hen of over 2.5 kilograms.

A Really Big Fish

One of the great thrills of angling is not knowing just when you are likely to hook a really big fish. Strangely, it is very common to actually underestimate their size, even when viewed at close quarters in the water.

Both Les and Howard Hill have landed a number of fish of over 4.5 kilograms while I have yet to achieve this milestone. Les and Howard both assert strongly that they had no idea of the true size of these magnificent specimens until they were actually in the net. For instance Les estimated the weight of a fish which weighed in at nearly five kilograms as nearer 2.5 until it was finally landed. This fish, incidentally, was weighed in the net and released. The brothers contend that there is no real way of telling, as often a four kilogram fish is the same length as one of only two or three kilograms.

However, there is one clue which may give an indication of a really big fish, according to Les. In his experience they do their fighting deep in the water, and as they are usually encountered in big pools they hug the bottom trying to elude capture. Larger fish usually fight with great doggedness rather than exhaust themselves with strength-sapping leaps. Again, according to Les, only when they are becoming very tired will they fight anywhere near the surface, and then they are likely to attempt to vacate the pool no matter how wild the rapid down into the next pool may be. These fish are usually the veterans of many floods, over a period of years, and are not fazed by being knocked around in a bit of white water.

If you suspect that you are into a much bigger than average fish it is fatal to try to rush things. This is where the patience which all anglers are supposed to possess becomes an essential quality. From time to time we are all "cleaned up" by unstoppable fish. With all the will in the world there is probably little that can be done in such circumstances, but put it down to experience, and admit defeat.

I never cease to be amazed at how the fighting characteristics of trout vary from one stream to another. One wonders if the fighting quality becomes endemic in trout of a particular environment. As I've said earlier, I believe that feeding and fighting peculiarities are directly related to the intrinsic nature of the water in which the fish dwell, and that both browns and rainbows, co-existing, tend not to vary too greatly in behaviour. I would qualify this belief somewhat by limiting the assertion to the more juvenile members of both species. Anyone who has hooked a really large brown at night knows that such a fish fights with an unyielding doggedness. By comparison the

Poor technique, lack of control in netting a fish.

rainbow, whether hooked during the hours of daylight or at night, spends quite a lot of time out of the water or near the surface.

While one could open an interesting debate on the fighting merits of browns compared to rainbows, this would serve little purpose in the context of this book. I do wonder, though, just what it is that causes the fish of one stream to behave so differently from those of another.

Some years ago I ventured into the upper reaches of the Wangapeka River for a couple of days of fairly leisurely fishing. I normally fish the lower and middle section where it runs through farmland and exotic forestry, so this little expedition, while not far from home, was quite novel all the same. From the end of the road at the Rolling River, the well-known Wangapeka Track to Little Wanganui on the West Coast begins, and it was the first part of the track that I ventured up a couple of hours before starting to fish, as I knew from past experience there that the road end section is fairly frequently fished.

I enjoyed my leisurely stroll upstream, savouring the scent of the dense beech forest and delighting in the song of tuis and bellbirds along the way. From time to time, where the river and track came close together I peered into the deep, mysterious pools trying to estimate the weights of the large but educated browns finning quietly on the bottom. At the bottom of a long, grassy slip, well known to local deer stalkers, I assembled my rod for the first time. Out of its protective cloth bag it came and I was in business.

In best commando fashion I began my stalk up through a series of pockets. I was soon rewarded by the sight of a small fish nymphing for all it was worth in the second significant pocket. It took the artificial

A big fish under control, coming to the net.

Good technique. Wide arm, high rod stance.

Netting head first.

without hesitation and cavorted all around the small pool for a few minutes before coming to the net, a fish of about one kilogram with a tiny head and thick body, resplendent in dozens of tiny spots of grey over a silver background. Released, it raced to sanctuary amongst the large, angular rocks at the base of the slip.

A similar fish performed in the same way a little further up, before the river changed character somewhat to run in a series of short, deep green pools. Big fish territory I mused, and was not surprised to spot a really good brown feeding well just below the surface near the top of the pool where the full force of the stream entered via a narrow chute of grey rock.

As I pondered the best plan of attack the fish made up my mind for me by rising nonchalantly to the surface to take an item of food right off the top. Without hesitation I changed over to a size 12 Molefly, at that time my favourite back country dry pattern. The gentlest of upstream breezes helped waft the fly up in front of the fish, and with hope in my heart I waited anxiously as the trout lifted perceptibly, actually nosed the fly and returned to its position. I tried again, this time with no response whatsoever. Without detailing the exact changes of flies, suffice to say that the trout continued to feed actively on naturals, but deigned to merely examine each new offering of mine.

Suspecting that drag could be the problem I warily changed casting position from time to time, still with the same total disdain from the fish. Time stood still as I methodically worked through my fly box, searching for the pattern which would break the spell. It must have been at least an hour later when without warning, on the umpteenth drift over the fish, it lifted its head above the surface and calmly clamped its jaws shut on a Black Gnat, a fly I'd had a singular lack of success with in the past.

I managed to react appropriately to set the hook, and then it was all on. Without the slightest hesitation the fish turned and ran straight towards me. Ignoring my presence it surged straight into the white water at the tail of the pool and into another, similar one and simply kept going. At this point it dawned on me that this fish was not going to slug it out on home ground. Desperately I tried to follow, slipping and sliding back and forth across the river. Still, it would not stop, try as I might to apply sidestrain. Finally we reached the pocket water where I'd begun fishing some hours earlier, and at last I was able to contain the still fit fish in the very pocket where I'd hooked and landed my first fish of the day. Once on a short line I was able to control the situation, and finally a near-exhausted angler netted a short, chunky fish weighing exactly 2.2 kilograms — no giant but a very good fish for the river.

I went on to land two more fish that day, both in the region of 1.5 kilograms as I recall. Both behaved in the same way as the fish I've just described. Though more easily controlled than the larger fish, the behaviour was virtually identical, with no inclination whatsoever to stay in the pool where they had been hooked. I've since had the same sort of experience on this river a number of times, especially in the narrow, upper reaches. What induces such a desire to vacate the home pool has me baffled, as I've discovered that in most streams with similar characteristics fish prefer to stay in one pool until things get really desperate.

About to beach a trout on fine gravel.

Remain In Touch

When trout behave in this way it is essential to remain in touch. To allow a fish to take a lot of line is courting disaster. If a trout decides that it is going only downstream the angler must react quickly and make an effort to follow. I once saw an acquaintance lose a very sizable fish by not making an attempt to follow as soon as it was obvious that it was not going to be easily stopped.

There is a decided advantage, in some situations, in having the fish forging upstream. Because the fish is tiring more quickly when fighting both angler and the strength of the current, the hook is more likely to retain a good hold through being driven back into the jaw. The tricky part is convincing the fish that it does actually want to go upstream. If the water below is not particularly suited to playing the fish it is worth making an effort to keep it going upstream, straining and tiring quite rapidly. To this end I have, on a few occasions, actually deliberately frightened the fish back upstream. This is a tactic to be employed sparingly though, and one fraught with a degree of peril as it is easy to panic the fish into a leader-snapping burst.

I've already mentioned the inclination of fish in bigger waters to tear headlong across the river towards the far bank. I've observed this idiosyncrasy on many occasions now, especially in relatively shallow stretches. The object seems to be for the trout to distance itself as quickly as possible from what would impede its actions. It is commonly stated that trout are not capable of feeling the pain of being hooked. While fish obviously do not feel pain as we mammals do, they must be aware of some discomfort as the hook takes hold. I don't believe that it is pain as such, probably more of an irritation which spurs the fish into action. They obviously find it unpleasant though, and to deny this is to delude ourselves. As much as anything, I believe it is the sudden weight of line and the feeling of restraint which induces the first panic-stricken dash away from the place where the strike took place.

On rare occasions fish which have been hooked briefly and lost will return to their niche and re-commence feeding. Rainbows are apt to do this a little more than browns. If you are fortunate enough to find yourself in this happy situation it is wise to exercise a little of that old patience and wait until the fish is really feeding actively again before trying to fool it again, and always with a different pattern of fly from that taken originally. This ploy has worked for me on quite a few occasions over the years, once even on a fish which I'd had on for some minutes. This particular brown can't have been too distressed by the first experience because it resumed feeding within seconds of getting rid of the first fly. It stayed on the second time too.

In summary, playing fish effectively means giving the fish its head when first hooked but, from then on, it requires a positive approach from the angler in order to achieve the objective of landing it as soon as possible. We have no right to torture fish on excessively light tippets or by allowing them to dictate terms. The old advice of keeping a tight line and "giving the fish the butt", i.e. applying sidestrain is very apt.

8

Landing And Releasing Fish

"The quality of mercy is not strained." So said Portia in *The Merchant of Venice.* Perhaps not. Still, the business of sparing trout to live and perhaps fight another day is very much the fashionable thing in angling circles, and for excellent reasons. I must admit to cringing when I view photographs of dead trout in quantity. Philip Holden's *The Golden Years of Fishing in New Zealand* is full of such scenes redolent of the great bison hunts of North America last century, or colonial days in Africa, the great white hunter posing with enormous quantities of game. While we can but marvel at the incredible size of the bags taken, and the average weight of the fish, there is something quite obscene about such depictions of greed. I've often wondered just how much waste of fish resulted, just to satisfy the egos of the victorious anglers.

Netting can be hazardous.

All this "holier than thou" stuff is not entirely justified. I still have in my possession a photograph depicting 15 dead trout, caught in one morning by myself and two other anglers. Certainly, not one fish was wasted, but still I look at it from time to time when I start to ascend my "high horse" to remind myself that angling is an evolutionary process. Most start at the "kill all" stage and eventually proceed through to the "release most" stage. The writers and many others have argued at length the wisdom of releasing trout, especially in more fragile environments where the fish stock is a very finite resource. Some guides now insist on a "catch and release" policy on the grounds that a superb back country trout is far too valuable to be caught only once. While I certainly applaud such a stance I am still firmly of the opinion that the taking of a trout for food, or as a trophy (Oh to be so lucky) is perfectly justifiable in virtually all circumstances. From time to time I enjoy eating trout, and sincerely trust that I shall always be able to do so.

On the other hand, if it is so decreed that certain waters cannot sustain "catch and kill", and are nominated "catch and release" only, I'll not object. I would welcome such a regulation on certain, small back country waters in my own beloved Nelson district.

It could be quite fairly argued that most rivers are capable of sustaining a total "catch and kill' regime as the brown trout, especially, is remarkably adept at holding its own against all that anglers can throw at it. However, the writers have observed an interesting trend in some of the smaller back country streams they fish on a regular basis each season.

Interest in trout fishing has burgeoned greatly in the last few years. In October and November stocks are excellent, replenished from the much larger main rivers during the close season. As the angling pressure intensifies during the summer months the fish available to the angler become fewer and fewer so that during February and March, prior to the spawning runs, the fishing is sometimes very hard indeed.

Now, it would be naive to assert that this phenomenon is entirely related to angling pressure. Other factors, including low water flows, could induce fish to move back into the sanctuary of the main river, or to simply seek out hiding places in the smaller stream. Without a properly researched study it would be unwise to jump to conclusions, but we are fairly well convinced that a large number of these fish are removed by anglers for good. The overall effect is not necessarily detrimental, except that these streams will harbour fewer and fewer of the very large trout for which they were once renowned.

There is absolutely no doubt in my mind that the average size of fish in headwater fisheries has declined significantly in the last ten years. As an example of this I cite the now heavily fished Leslie River of North-West Nelson. I have said it before, and I repeat the contention, that some parts of this river must rank amongst the most heavily fished in the district during the summer months, despite the fact that it is a full day's walk from the nearest roadhead. At the height of the season a number of tramping and fishing parties per day travel the track alongside the river which links with the Wangapeka Track a few days walk away. Members of many of these groups fish the river, and the lucky ones take their catch to supplement their dehydrated food. Despite a monumental flood in October 1988 there

Poor technique, rough handling of fish.

are still reasonable numbers of fish in the river, but the very large fish, commonplace in the sixties and seventies, are all but gone.

Natural disasters aside, I contend that the principal reason for this is "catch and kill". A voluntary policy of "catch and release", or at least extremely low daily bag limits, may be necessary on such streams. Contentious though it may be, I would personally favour a one fish per day limit on virtually all South Island headwater fisheries, and would urge that the very top sections of some streams, at least, be set aside for "catch and release" only.

As our contribution to this effort, Les Hill and I will not take fish from certain tributary streams unless it is that one in a thousand "trophy trout", and even then simply attaining the magic 4.5 kilogram status does not necessarily destine it to that space above the fireplace. Les has returned a number of "double figure" fish in recent seasons.

As we have said in *Stalking Trout* food fish should come from the ranks of smaller, more abundant fish, and preferably from larger waters, thereby enhancing angling opportunities on the little back country gems for much more than perhaps two months of the year. There is no doubting that increasing affluence is leading to greater mobility and a dramatic upsurge in interest in solitary, "back to nature" recreational pursuits such as angling. In the forseeable future we must either adopt a conscious conservation policy or see the quality of our angling inevitably decline.

Attitudes to many things are changing. Recently I saw a heartening example of a changing attitude which gave me great heart, and faith in the younger generation, at a time when it is fashionable to criticise the actions of youth.

I'd arranged to meet well-known angler, Norman Marsh, at the Alexander Bluff bridge on the Motueka one fine Sunday in the middle of the 1988/89 season.

An ideal fish for the pot.

"I want to show you some tricky little devils up under the willows," he chuckled over the phone. "Meet me at 10 o'clock."

At the duly appointed time I was standing on the aforementioned bridge gazing into the low, clear Motueka. For all intents and purposes it had the appearance of a fishless desert as I could see every stone and granite crevice on the bottom. Apart from one portly brown parading around a set beat at the western side of the bridge there wasn't a fish in sight. Still, the swallows were active and I marvelled at their glorious iridescent plumage as they dashed and darted under the bridge snatching small mayflies and the small delta-winged passionfruit hoppers.

I was startled out of my reverie by the strident call of a kea, obviously enjoying a holiday in the low country. As I glanced up two teenage boys wandered on to the eastern end of the bridge. Sensibly clad in olive green jerseys and shorts they shuffled listlessly along, rods in hand. By their very demeanour I realised that they were not meeting with much success. We chatted awhile, and I learned that they were camped nearby, and had spent the weekend fishing in the vicinity. Their spinning rods gave a clue to their singular lack of

111

success. Spinning for browns in a low mid-summer Motueka, except perhaps for a brief period around dawn or dusk, is about as productive as running on the spot. Sadly, one of the lads informed me he'd broken the tip of his grandfather's split cane fly rod, and wasn't looking forward to revealing this little gem to him.

At that moment Norman came stumping onto the bridge armed with rod and vest. He wasn't exactly in the best humour. Apparently his motor scooter had run out of fuel a kilometre or so down the road. Norman suspected it'd been siphoned in the night. Not an auspicious start.

I told him of the boys' lack of success, and he generously suggested that they tag along with us. The ill omens had been cast though, and the fish did nothing to brighten the day up. Two hours later Norman and I had both lost fish and spooked one or two as well.

Dame Fortune smiled finally when I spied a fine fish feeding in a nice riffly stretch. Perhaps I was nervous, due to my audience, but it took quite a few casts and changes of fly before I induced a take to a less than perfectly presented dry fly of Norman's creation. As soon as it was clear that the fish was well hooked Norman suggested

Returning trout to the water.

that I let one of the boys land it. Somewhat reluctantly one of the pair assumed the task. The fish played hard to get, diving time and again for the only snag, a long willow branch lying on the stream bed. Finally, in a flurry of muddy water I netted a very fine trout of around 1.6 kilograms.

"Would you like it?" I asked the youngster whose name now eludes me. "You could take it home with you tonight.'

I might as well have made an obscene suggestion as a very firm, "No thank you," came simultaneously from both lads. "We'd like to see you let it go," said one, so with no further ado I flipped the hook out with a pair of surgical forceps and slid the fat hen fish out of the enveloping folds of the net. The lady soon regained her composure and swayed off gracefully into the current. Now, I must admit to being rather flabbergasted by such generosity, and I could see that Norman was also suitably impressed as well.

Being totally honest I must admit to the fact that I would have taken that fish home had I been on my own as it was in splendid condition. Later I received a modicum of gentle ribbing from my wife who'd placed an order for a fish for dinner.

This little example serves, I hope, to illustrate a certain development of maturity amongst New Zealand trout fishing buffs. I know only too well that Taupo attitudes have a long way to go, and that the only logical way to reduce the take in that fishery is to legislate to reduce daily bag limits, thereby protecting the fish hogs from themselves.

One can argue the pros and cons of "catch and release" until the cows come home. Even if it is practised by all anglers, once they have developed a degree of proficiency in the sport, the fishery generally will benefit.

In recent years I've read a number of articles relating to the release of trout. A common theory, and not a very popular one because it pricks the consciences of anglers, is that releasing trout is pointless for the fish is doomed anyway due to the stress of being played and a subsequent build-up of lactic acid in the flesh which results in a condition somewhat akin to muscle cramp in humans. If this is so then it would be difficult to justify angling as a sport, purely on the grounds of cruelty, and it is such a stance which is now being adopted by the animal rights groups.

Other research though, indicates that larger fish especially are able to happily survive the rigours of hooking, playing, landing and release as long as they are landed quickly and released with care. It is not only to assuage my conscience that I subscribe to this latter theory. All New Zealand professional guides adhere to the policy of "catch and release" for their careers depend on it. I've taken the time to speak to a number of these professionals who personally release hundreds of trout per year, many, many more than the average recreational angler. Without exception they insist that carefully released fish do survive.

How do they know this? Some of the expert South Island guides regularly cover the same water, and soon recognise characteristics of individual fish. From experience they know every brown trout has qualities which distinguish it from its fellows. These subtle but distinctive differences may take the form of colouring, size, shape, condition and unusual jaw shape, scar, or may be related to the fish's niche or feeding pattern. So convinced are the guides that they are dealing with the same obliging quarry that they assign names to their old friends. I've done this myself. On six successive occasions I tried for a trout on the upper Motueka. It had a distinctive black tail. ''Old Blacktail'' finally fell to a size 12 Molefly one Sunday morning, and after a dingdong battle I landed it in the next pool downstream. The following weekend it was back cruising its usual beat.

I'm convinced that released trout survive, and we must all believe that implicitly or kill everything we catch, a practice which reduces us to crass pot hunters.

I wince when I see some people release trout.

In the past some of the charter boat operators on Lake Taupo have been somewhat careless about the way they returned under sized fish. Hopefully, now they are better informed about the consequences of simply throwing fish back from a considerable height.

Guiding Principles

I've also seen stream anglers do it all wrong too. There is a right and a wrong way to do everything, and releasing fish carefully is not easy. Below are a few guiding principles gleaned from experience, some of which we will examine in detail:

Good technique.
Gentle return of fish.

1. Adopt the use of barbless hooks.
2. Avoid unnecessary "playing".
3. Use the strongest practicable tippet.
3. Beach fish only on a gently sloping sand or fine shingle beach, and walk the fish ashore by applying firm, steady pressure. Avoid winding fish in as this seems to panic them more.
5. Never allow a fish which is intended for release to thrash around on rough ground or very dry surfaces.
6. Use a wide-mouthed landing net.
7. Avoid hand contact if possible, or else ensure that hands are wet.
8. Avoid touching gills, pressing the abdomen firmly or dislodging large areas of scales.
9. Remove the hook quickly and cleanly with surgical forceps or a similar instrument.
10. Hold the fish in an inverted position while removing the hook as this lessens the struggling.
11. Hold the fish in the current to revive it but do not move it backwards and forwards.

It's a long list I know, but all things being equal the fish will survive its ordeal. Releasing a trout whilst fishing alone is frequently a difficult procedure, especially if the bank topography is steep or overhanging branches intrude. Probably the worst possible scenario is a combination of circumstances which results in some sort of impasse.

I recall vividly such an experience on the Wangapeka some years ago. I'd hooked a strong fish which, in typical Wangapeka fashion, tore off downstream into an enormous pool of great depth. I resigned myself to a break-off, as try as I might, I simply could not reach the fish with my short-handled net. Time and time again I drew thc fish

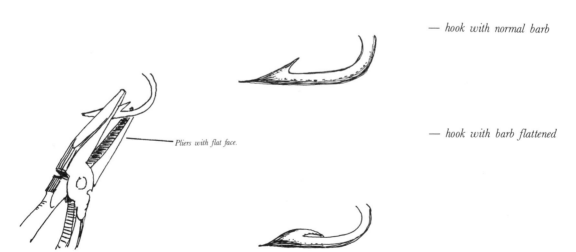

— *hook with normal barb*

Pliers with flat face.

— *hook with barb flattened*

Squashing the barb on a hook

to the point where the rapid broke into the top of the big pool. I could go no further and I feared that drawing the leader into the rod rings would result in an over-stressed tippet. Each time I drew the fish into the rapid it used the current to mount another run well down into the big green pool.

After perhaps 20 minutes or so of this I finally took the bull by the horns and wound the long leader right onto the reel, whereupon I was finally able to scoop the near-exhausted fish up with my rather inadequate net. It took a while to revive but, when released, swam off, seemingly unscathed. The whole business would have been made immeasurably easier if I'd been fishing with a partner, with the fish being netted and released in a few minutes.

However, there are times when an enthusiastic assistant netter is far more of a hindrance than help. Many experienced anglers insist on netting fish themselves but, personally, I don't care too much one way or the other. The object is simply to land the fish as quickly as possible. If my angling companion asks me to land a fish for him I'm happy to oblige. On one occasion though, much younger, and somewhat wet behind the ears in terms of angling experience, I was partially, at least, responsible for losing a mate's very large trout. We had spotted this leviathan in a tiny stream, and even more amazingly from a main road bridge. Ho promptly deceived it with a small Pheasant Tail nymph, but was quite unprepared for the strength of the fish. After racing round and round the tiny pool an impasse developed with the trout firmly stuck in mid-current.

Our greenness was our undoing. After five minutes or so I decided to try to net the fish. The water in the three metre wide stream was much deeper than it appeared, and I was quickly up to my waist in the ice cold, snow fed spate. Foolishly I slid the net up from the tail, and received quite a shock when I could only fit half the fish in. I made a desperate attempt to scoop the monster up but succeeded only in trying the fish's patience just too far. It surged upstream and under a submerged log before the inevitable break-off occurred. Now much older and wiser I'm well aware that I should have left well alone and waited for natural attrition in the form of steady, unrelenting pressure to take its toll before any attempt at netting. Just to disturb a few more sacred cows I will assert my preference for headfirst netting, especially of larger trout.

Beaching, rather than netting, has already been mentioned. This method has much to commend it as I've seen many fish lost through inept netting attempts. A partner can still prove invaluable by quietly removing the hook and releasing the fish while it is still held on a tight line by the angler. I firmly believe that a beached fish is less stressed than a netted one, especially if it is simply allowed to flop over on its side in shallow water. Repeated stabs with a landing net serve only to induce a high state of apprehension and panic in the fish.

When netting it is imperative that the angler does not move around excessively when the fish is approaching the net. Attempt to position the fish so that it is moving in a slow, controlled fashion downstream

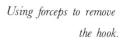

Using forceps to remove the hook.

towards the angler. Hold the net in the current with the bag flowing back downstream. Should the fish be alarmed by the angler, careful positioning will result in the fish bolting, one hopes, into the enveloping folds of the net. If it swims past it is better to bring it around for another attempt rather than make blind stabs or to pursue it downstream. Of course the fish must be ''played'' to a point where it is not likely to make a leader-snapping run across the river. Patience and quiet, unhurried movements are vital.

Carrying a trout carefully.

Long Leaders

The long leaders which we are forced to use to deceive trout can also be a real curse to the upstream angler. Most methods of securing leader to floating line inevitably result in at least some form of possible impediment to the smooth flow of line through the top ring of the rod. Many anglers have lost fish because of the sudden stoppage of the line just as the fish is about to be landed or netted. Most sports shops will whip the leader to the floater and apply a coating of smooth varnish. Many anglers, especially if they are rod makers or fly tiers, do it for themselves. Still others swear by the use of Super-glue and poke the butt section of the leader into the core of the floating line. This works well and provides a wonderful connection. The only reservation I have is that Super-glue has the disadvantage of failing quite suddenly and unexpectedly. To date though all the anglers I know who use this method report complete satisfaction. They do insist that the link should be checked before each outing, something we should do anyway.

I used to use small leader links of tapered plastic and found these quite satisfactory most of the time though I did encounter the odd problem of sticking. At any rate, exercise extreme care once the leader is inside the rings, as on such a short line there is not as much "give" to absorb a particularly strong run.

I would rather lose my fly in the fish's jaw than handle the fish excessively. Just occasionally one finds oneself in such a position that it is virtually impossible to land a fish without causing it unnecessary suffering or even jeopardising its chances of survival.

On our last back country trip, Les Hill was forced to deliberately break the leader on one occasion as he was waist deep in a long scrub-lined section of river with vertical banks on either side. While he felt that he could have eventually netted the fish he chose to give it its freedom by snapping the leader. As we use barbless hooks almost exclusively now it would not be long before the fish managed to rid itself of the fly. All research I've read on the subject indicates that trout do indeed have little difficulty in ridding themselves of hooks, usually within a day or so.

If it is possible to avoid any handling of the fish, or contact with

The big ones should go back.

Placing a trout gently into a stream — facing upstream.

118

dry ground, so much the better. It is believed that handling of the gills usually results in the death of the fish. Excessive constriction of the stomach area can also prove fatal.

Some scales are inevitably lost as a trout is netted. As long as this scale loss is not excessive it will not harm it, according to Fisheries Research Scientist, Don Jellyman. Large areas of scale loss could, however place extra stresses on the fish by providing a site for infection.

Only recently I learned that a trout will struggle less if held in an inverted position while the hook is being removed. I must admit to being somewhat dubious about this contention, but when I put theory into practice on a trip in 1988 I found that, while it does not obviate the struggles altogether, it does make a significant difference at a time when speed is essential in order to ensure survival.

Placing a fish into the water, with its head facing upstream.

When I first began releasing trout, well over a decade ago now, I was under the mistaken impression that it was necessary to move the fish vigorously back and forth in the water. Little did I realise then that I was in fact slowly drowning the poor creature. In retrospect then it is somewhat surprising that so many of them did actually swim off of their own volition after this rather tough treatment. The fish simply needs to be held in water, cradled gently and held upright. When it is ready it will swim off quite happily.

There is no doubt that a trout is stressed to quite a high degree by being played, landed and released, and oddly, the fish which has thrashed around in the net so violently only seconds before release is sometimes apt to simply lie doggo in the water upon return to the river. Keep an eye on such fish as often they appear to lose their equilibrium and may even flop on their sides or turn belly up. A sign that all is not well is when the fish goes quite rigid with the body forming the shape of a curve. If left in this position they may not survive. Often, all that is required to stir the fish to action is to actually scare it with a splash nearby or to give it a gentle poke with the rod tip. Such procedures may seem a little excessive but they do seem to have the desired effect. We must not lose sight of the fact that the object of the exercise is to restore the fish to full strength as soon as possible.

9

Concentration

Although it was well over a decade ago the memory of shooting my first deer is still quite clear. Beyond the shot lies a void, but the moments prior, when attention, senses, instincts all became totally preoccupied, remains vivid.

In those days, in the mid-seventies, some deer still grazed bush edges. In the evening, as darkness approached they'd emerge from scrub and bush drawn by greener pastures, stray from their leafy cloak, knowing darkness allowed even better cover. But in that short space of time, in the twilight, a hunter had his best chance.

My lookout was carefully chosen. I sat right on the bush edge, on a high shoulder, looking down an ever-tumbling stream. It flowed through a long, narrow clearing, a tongued indent into the bush. At least 200 metres below the natural bush line, it was an ideal evening grazing ground, less exposed yet grassed and watered. This was mid-February. For weeks, even in the mountains, skies had remained clear. The bush, ever thirsty, lay wanting. Yet, overhead the first promise of a dowsing showed. Up the hillside rolled a thin misty shroud, dampening the canopy, reaching down to exposed tussocks but nowhere touching the earth. A mist, light drizzle perhaps — no more.

For an hour I sat, facing the breeze, peering down the clearing, down the stream, waiting. An uphill breeze — ideal, because if I had to stalk downhill it would be into the wind. Well, almost. The mist rolling over the tree tops and into the clearing swirled somewhat, reached down, ducked sideways and at times climbed back.

How it got there I know not. I saw no hints at all, not a movement. Inattentive probably. But, suddenly, a stag, with a majestic head of developing antlers, grazed fully 50 metres away from the bush. Now that it was sighted it stood obvious, a red-brown against green.

Instantly more alert I considered the possibilities. A shot from where I lay? Too far with my open sighted .303. Wait for the beast to graze closer? Darkness crept nearer quickly, no time for that. The only other alternative — stalk closer myself, creep through tinder dry bush, risk a swirling breeze but be secure from sight in the darkening bush. A hundred metres to travel. Fifteen minutes to do so. Fifteen minutes tuned absolutely to breeze, sound and reaching ahead with my eyes, 15 minutes of total concentration. They were as exciting as a man could wish. I marvelled at the completeness of the twig covering, every step, ever so carefully placed, broke something. Mosses, browned and parched crunched menacingly; branches reached down everywhere, brushed and rustled against arms and legs. Taking a line deep in the bush I could not see the deer. This way

I figured, if I couldn't see him, he couldn't see me. "Head downhill for 70 metres," I thought, "then crawl across to the clearing."

As I eased closer to open ground and strayed towards the verge of my shadowy cover I expected to find the deer gone. Had I been too noisy? Then there was my scent. Being so close now any swirling breeze would carry my presence in moments and spark an instant retreat. Right at the bush edge, a huge tree lay fallen, ancient, infested with moss and lichen, felled by the wind no doubt. I crawled up to it, poked the rifle barrel ahead and ever so slowly, lifted my head to look out. At first nothing. Then, a small movement, then a massive shuddering rump and flanks. The stag signalled its presence by spraying millions of droplets of water from its coat, sending a shower high and wide. Then the head came up. Testing the breeze? I remained frozen. Out of sight. Absolutely silent, tuned now to odour. Ironically I could smell the beast, musky and pungent.

Solitude established, the animal's head went down again, to graze once more. That was its last act.

I didn't aim for the head or neck particularly — just the biggest bit. I didn't squeeze the trigger but pulled it quickly. At the same time I'm sure both eyes closed and the brass-plated butt thumped into my shoulder. Yet, somehow, I succeeded. The stag just sank from where it stood. From within me emerged momentary elation but the remorse that followed grew quickly. The animal lay dead. I'd destroyed the centre of my attention, the focus that for 15 minutes had allowed me to tune closely with the bush. Such intense concentration in hunting is widely accepted; in fact it's paramount to success. It's the same with many other sports and pastimes. Chess players need it, as do pale-faced pool players, archers, sprinters and so on. Losing it leads to diminished performance.

How different the view of fishermen. Fishing! Synonymous with relaxation, with feet up, brain neutralised, motion minimised. Who could be critical of this? Certainly not me. For the majority of fishermen it will always be so. They'll always be happy even if they rarely catch fish. Got one last season, well remembered, often recalled.

But there is another view. I remember reading once the writings of a most successful fly angler who caught trout on every outing. He said that he always fished alone. He had to because fishing involved so much concentration.

Maybe the two perspectives are not so far apart. Distant perhaps in result, distant too in action, but equally relaxing. One angler is relaxing through inertness, the other through total preoccupation of mind and soul. But there is no doubt that if it is your intention to catch trout a high level of concentration is needed.

In this book our intention has been to guide anglers, by highlighting common pitfalls, towards greater success. It is our duty therefore, to maintain a consistent direction and advocate a single-minded approach of high concentration in all that is done.

While the essence of our story revolves around the sequence of events involved in capture, from locating a fish to its ultimate netting, the need for concentration begins much earlier. It is in the seeking of trout, the stalking, that initial concentration is essential. Actively stalking trout involves two overriding objectives — first an angler must try to maintain concealment himself and secondly, of course, he must locate feeding fish. The two are inevitably entwined.

A trout's greatest defence is its eyesight. It sees equally well near and far, detects colour and most of all is infinitely perceptive of even subtle movement. Aware of this, a bank-bound angler has a focus for his concentration. Wearing appropriate clothing of subtle tones is an obvious advantage. Movement, usually upstream, should be slow, very slow. It is commonly known that fast-moving objects, through the contrast they provide, are most obvious. Slow a body's speed, particularly one blending with its surrounds, and it becomes more difficult to detect. Where possible, an angler can slip from cover to cover — a gorse bush, long grass, shrubbery — peering over, through, around. Elsewhere, if such advantage is not present, where a bank or beach is free of vegetation, it may be possible to walk further from the water's edge or even stick close to back cover, tall shrubs or trees behind.

While stalking I employ three defensive ploys. I move as slowly as possible, I stay as far from the water's edge as I can while still having a good view into the water and I search as far upstream as I can, hoping to locate fish while still out of their most perceptive forward or side-on vision.

Eyes On The Water

Looking for trout is a more offensive role, and one which requires infinite concentration. One principle stands paramount in the search — an angler must keep his eyes waterwards. It has been my observation that the vast majority of stalking anglers do not concentrate enough. They're continually distracted, keeping their eyes appropriately focused on the water for only a surprisingly small percentage of the time. The greatest distraction is foot-watching, searching for the easiest, least cumbersome path along the bank. At times to redirect your eyes to that purpose is essential — but stop while doing so and refocus on the water before moving on. At other times, if forward movement is slow enough, an angler can feel his way with his feet and use subtle peripheral vision and so maintain his stare where it should be.

I've written before about the idea of selective vision when actively stalking. We all experience and constantly practise selective hearing. We direct our hearing to radio voices or music and eliminate peripheral sound. Selective vision operates similarly and is essential to successful stalking. To keep one's eyes on the water is the first level of concentration, but continual success, particularly in broken water, requires a greater commitment, reaching with the eyes through the water to the bed, searching for contrasts of movement, tone, colour, shape, line. Beyond the commitment lies a belief, a positive attitude that there are fish to be seen and that you will see them.

Once a trout has been located, the defensive ploys of remaining undetected must be maintained, even heightened. It is at this stage a multitude of signals are conveyed to the trout — waving rods, flashing fly boxes, pointing, movements of many sorts. At the same time the offensive strategy must be maintained too. The immediate problems involve approaching the best casting position stealthily. This assumes, of course, consideration of possible line control difficulties on the water and inevitable casting obstacles particularly behind and ahead. All of this observation should be done while maintaining, where at all possible, direct, uninterrupted visual contact with the fish or, in less favourable light, an exact knowledge of where the fish was seen, and hopefully still lies. None of this should be guesswork.

It is at this point that so many new fly fishers effectively lose fish long before they're hooked. There seems to be a lack of appreciation of the need to know exactly where the fish is. This knowledge is required so that casting length, direction and action can be monitored and trout responses be observed. While an angler is engaged in active pursuit he must concentrate on the fish but, to add to his problems, he must also be aware exactly where his fly is, whether it be in the air or on the water. In fact once the fly has settled waterwards that's where direct focus should be centred, waiting, hoping deceit will be achieved. Without his eyes on the fly an angler cannot observe the take and therefore cannot time his strike, the essence of successful hooking.

Fishing a nymph requires similar levels of concentration although the technique being employed will determine whether fish, nymph, line or indicator should be watched. Whatever the case, wherever the attention, the commitment remains unchanged.

An angler lacking positive attitudes, devoid of concentration, is not pitting his wits, his skill and perception against those of the trout. Instead it's a matter of luck against instinct. On the Oreti backwaters, with high angler traffic, glassy surfaces and wide open approaches, luck is inevitably unreliable.

The Oreti River has never been a favourite of mine, many other streams hold greater attractions. But along its margins this river boasts some fine backwaters. Connected, yet separate from the mainstream, these all house trout — cruisers, bottom feeders, surface sippers, ever mobile, ever watchful, super-selective trout. These waters, pond-like or gently flowing, seem to have a similarity in configuration. Occupying river bed margins they are flanked, on the rural side, by dense willow growth. On the river side, the angler's approach, there are open gravel beaches, swept clear of vegetation. Sometimes, at best, a low grassy bank may offer some comfort — marginal cover, no more.

Confronted by an open bed I approached such a backwater several years ago. Backed by a tangled mass of greenery, the still waters ahead lay clear, exposed to the bed. A stable mud bed supported healthy clumps of cress and denser stands of elodea each reaching surfacewards in 40 centimetres of water, deeper certainly along the far bank, beneath the haven of willow roots.

I stopped a considerable distance back, searched for movement, a shape beneath or a surface ripple. Right on the edge, where a narrow channel had been carved, a shape eased along, stopped, nudged the bed, lifted to the surface, then drifted left and right selecting food at will. Although I was eager to move forward, an uneasy constraint prevailed — a hope of observing a feeding path, a territorial beat.

There are times when, having exercised patience and appropriate vigilance, one wishes at the end of it all that spontaneity had prevailed. Maturity, reason, experience here had built a mountain of difficulties. The greatest was that to effect a cast I had to position myself, without cover, in full view of the trout as it emerged from the deep and approached my edge. Then, if I remained unseen I had to wait for my adversary to move away far enough along the edge before casting. For some time during its beat the trout disappeared from view and sought the deeper waters. That was when I stooped waterwards then, cursing the discomfort of gravel bruising my knees, waited. From my new position, closer now to the feeding lane, the trout as it approached appeared bigger than before. Nearer and nearer it came looking directly at me. Then, suddenly it was gone. When a highly distressed fish turns and darts for cover the swivel isn't seen, nor the initial metres covered, just the cloud of mud and the surface swirl. The acceleration is terrific.

I doubt that that fish reasoned what lay ahead — just sensed an object had appeared, one that hadn't been there on the hundred previous beats and shouldn't be there now.

Losing but not defeated, I vowed to return the next week to try again. This time I positioned myself a little further back, tried to lie inert and offer a lower profile. But the result was the same. These trout know every feature of their niche, every line of the horizon beyond. My back, however prone, did not belong. Now there lay the answer. If I remained where I crouched for long enough, sooner or later I'd become familiar, accepted. That wasn't possible but not far away, a clump of gorse, uprooted during a recent fresh, lay bare. I dragged it towards the backwater and left it, like a hide, right where I wished to cast from. For a week it stayed there, all the time growing familiar, disdained at first maybe, I know not, but ''growing'' into the niche.

The scene remained unchanged when I returned. The gorse clump, my cover, lay prone, unmoved. A few metres beyond, the trout fed as before. Three times now I'd been there yet strangely the fish had not yet been tempted. This time. If a breeze blew that day it certainly did not reach down to me. In the stillnes it became possible to lay a fly out on the feeding path while the fish swam from view. The trap set, the wait commenced. A tiny dry, an 18 I think, blessed with hope, sat upright.

It would be easy to say, ''Like clockwork the fish appeared and eased towards the fly . . .'', but it wasn't so. An eel, not threatening in its size but an intruder still, weaved among the cress. Directly above, a damselfly pair performed their mating dance, resting momentarily where leaf and water met. It wasn't until my senses had relaxed, cramped limbs complaining, that the fish showed. My eyes travelled from fly to trout then trout to fly, willing the two to converge more quickly. Tiny flies, like the naturals they imitate, must appear more attractive to fish. Their use engenders a confidence. I knew the trout would rise. And so it did. Not high — in shallow water, that was unnecessary. The nose broke clear, the fly disappeared.

I paused the angler's eternal two seconds. The trout levelled. As my knuckles whitened, left hand tensed, my right elbow began lifting a tiny dry fly popped onto the water's surface just behind the trout's head, above its back. How the lift was stopped I cannot recall, it's such a reflex action. The trout drifted on, undisturbed.

Concentration. This time rewarded, another chance allowed. The fly retrieved, it was replaced by an equally tiny, unweighted nymph. The trap was set again. This time, as the concentric rings of the lake widened, the nylon began to straighten and dip towards the fish. I lifted strongly. At last a tight line.

Had I failed that time I don't know whether I would have returned. That matters little. What remains important here is the basis of success. To me intense concentration and precise visual contact with fish and fly brought the ultimate reward.

At times like this it is pertinent to reflect on the remorse felt after succeeding in a deer stalk. With trout, their territory, their domain can be entered, disturbed somewhat after the deceit and during the battle, but most satisfyingly complete destruction is not necessary. A trout, unlike a deer, can be returned to freedom.

The Last Cast

Les Hill began this book by referring to the importance of "getting it right", first time. As the honour of penning the final statement in this book has been bestowed on me, I would like to take a more philosophical view of things, away from the hard practicalities of casting, controlling line and playing fish, for instance.

Throughout the book we have attempted to "lighten" the text by way of anecdote, and by referring to an imaginary, inexperienced angler, beset by the problems which we all experience from time to time, especially as we make those first enthusiastic but frustrating steps into the world of upstream angling for trout. We sincerely hope that our anecdotes and experiences gleaned in over 50 years of combined time spent fly fishing have served their purpose.

We hope too that the book does not come across as "the definitive work" on the subject. As mentioned earlier, there is really not much very new in the world of fly fishing for trout. As we see it innovation in terms of equipment is the only area where really major changes are likely to occur. The actual method and style of fishing is likely to change little. Sure, fads will come and go and old methods be revisited, but trout are trout, and they are not likely to change.

I have been able to empathise greatly with the unfortunate, imaginary angler referred to from time to time, as I have certainly "been there" myself. Unlike Les Hill I did not come from a fishing or hunting background, though I have always been passionately dedicated to both these sports, and was fortunate enough to have a few mentors along the way.

Regrettably though I did not really experience fly fishing proper until I was through my teenage years. The youngster introduced to fly fishing at a tender age has a wonderful advantage, as young people have open minds, uncluttered by pre-conceived notions and are flexible enough to adapt to new and different ideas as they are presented.

Fly fishing did not come easily to me. While I was wildly enthusiastic and determined to an almost obsessional degree to become reasonably proficient, it was still hard going, operating largely independently, and in something of a void, aided only by the books I could lay my hands on from time to time.

Books did help by at least pointing me in the right direction, and it is in that spirit that I suggest this book be approached, not as an angling "Bible", but rather as food for thought for beginner and old stager alike. The writers believe that there is a place for such a book, with its rather detailed analysis of some aspects normally glossed over. The book did not just happen, and to our ever-patient publisher's near despair has been some years in the making.

I have alluded briefly to the frustrations of fly fishing, particularly when fishing for browns in less than perfect conditions. I've spent at least some part of the last three days in the company of an angler who has met with more than his share of the frustration I've been referring to.

John is one of those people who has only recently discovered fly fishing. Being able to visit the Tongariro River on many occasions during the winter has meant that he has enjoyed success virtually from the outset, literally from the time he learned to cast a reasonably long line with his weight 9 graphite rod. Fishing weighted nymphs through some of the upper pools of the Tongariro has produced great results these last two or three winters, including a number of limit bags. Fantastic fishing, I'm sure you'll agree.

John has done very little fishing for browns, though, and had taken his first on a dry fly just weeks before his visit to the Motueka. This milestone had whetted the appetite, so when an opportunity presented itself John and his wife decided to spend a long weekend with friends in the Motueka Valley. While Kay enjoyed the potteries and other craft outlets in the district John attacked the river at every opportunity.

The weekend was enjoyable in every possible way, apart from the fact that not one fish was landed in many hours of fishing. To be fair, even old hands on the river were finding the going tough. It did not help that the annual invasion of anglers from outside the district was in full swing. This meant that every good pool or run had fishermen through it every day. The brown is a fish which simply will not tolerate this extra disturbance, and is inclined to retire to safe havens.

Compared with only a few weeks previous the evening hatches were virtually non-existent, and in three successive evenings of fishing both wet and dry fly until after dark I succeeded in landing only a solitary fish each evening, very poor by local standards.

All right, John was up against it, but there were other difficulties as well, which he was only too happy to acknowledge as the weekend progressed. He had difficulty spotting fish when stalking upstream during the day, and even when fish were pointed out to him he had the utmost difficulty in pinpointing their position with accuracy. During the winter runs of rainbows the ability to spot fish in the Tongariro or Tauranga-Taupo is not a high priority, but in high midsummer on a South Island brown trout stream this is an essential skill.

But to my mind John had other difficulties which conspired against him, more important than the ability to spot, for I was able to seek out fish for him. No, his major problems related to some of the areas we have covered at length in this book, such things as casting with a tight loop so that not too much line is thrown high in the air, a dead giveaway to wary browns. I noted too a tendency for the nymph to make contact with the water with a splash, and for the leader not to straighten to its full length. These and other aspects of line control in the air and on the water combined to make life difficult for John. And to add insult to injury, when he did succeed in hooking the best trout seen one day, it broke him off under a submerged log just when it appeared to be under control.

Such is life, and I'm happy to report that far from being despondent, John declared the weekend a great success making him even more determined to gain a greater degree of proficiency. I expect to see him back in the not too distant future, and certainly better prepared.

Throughout this book we have stressed the need to apply concentration to the task at hand. Heightened powers of awareness combined with a positive attitude ultimately bring results. Perhaps, at times this book has stressed the serious side to a point where it may be thought that the writers gain little pleasure from what they are doing. Nothing could be further from the truth. While there is a desire to constantly improve one's performance there is plenty of time for the light-hearted banter and ribbing which is also part and parcel of the angling experience.

I've dwelt at some length on the attitude to losing a fish. This normally results in the angler having to endure a certain amount of leg pulling, until of course, it happens to someone else. We enjoy our time on the river. Without a doubt, there are some more forgettable days. My personal pet hate is retracing one's steps down a rough river bed after perhaps ten or 12 hours of forging on upstream, around "Just one more bend". Les is very much inclined to drag me on just that little bit further when I have visions of nothing but a cold beer, a hot meal and a long, dreamless sleep in mind.

This urge to go further than we have ever gone before up back country rivers in particular, is very strong. There is something tremendously exciting about entering totally new water for the first time. On our last trip we did this. Les almost had to be physically forced to turn back at 7.30 pm, and it was a very tired group of anglers who arrived back at the camp site sometime after 10 o'clock.

We must never lose sight of the fact that angling for trout is a recreational pastime. The Concise Oxford Dictionary defines recreation as to "refresh, entertain or agreeably occupy". I have a strong suspicion that some anglers lose sight of this and bring the sport into the realms of a competitive activity. The writers have long regarded angling competitions as somewhat alien to angling, and I for one will not even enter my local club competition each year. Still, each to their own. If competition is found enjoyable, and, providing conservation values are not threatened, then there is probably no great harm done.

Angling can develop a great sense of camaraderie, especially when reliant on the good nature of one's companions on extended trips into the back country, where one person's selfishness or ill-humour may spoil things for the whole group. We have dwelt on this aspect at some length in our earlier book, *Stalking Trout*. It certainly makes good sense to choose one's companions carefully. Good relationships stand the test of time. Poor ones don't.

In conclusion, spare a thought for the fish. Without the forethought of a small band of British settlers our rivers would be barren places. We owe them plenty for providing the sport we now enjoy. It behoves us to treat our quarry with respect and dignity. If a fish is to be killed for food or as trophy it should be done swiftly and cleanly. If it is to be returned, this should be effected with skill and care.

References

''Flycasting.'' George Ferris 1977
Published by William Heinemann Ltd

''Trout.'' Ernest Schwiebert 1979
Published by Andre Deutsch — London

''Nymphs and the Trout.'' Frank Sawyer 1981
Published by A C Black — London

''Trout With Nymph.'' Tony Orman 1974
Published by Hodder and Stroughton Ltd

''Trout on a Nymph.'' Tony Orman 1991
Published by The Halcyon Press

''The Golden Years of Fishing in NZ.'' Philip Holden 1984
Published by Hodder and Stroughton Ltd

''The Trout and the fly.'' Brian Clarke & John Goddard 1980
Published by Ernest Benn Ltd

''In the Ring of the Rise.'' Vincent C. Marinaro 1976
Published by Crown Publishers, Inc New York